Forever in Thy Path

Forever in Thy Path

The God of Black Liberation

HARRY H. SINGLETON III

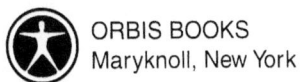
ORBIS BOOKS
Maryknoll, New York

Founded in 1970, Orbis Books endeavors to publish works that enlighten the mind, nourish the spirit, and challenge the conscience. The publishing arm of the Maryknoll Fathers and Brothers, Orbis seeks to explore the global dimensions of the Christian faith and mission, to invite dialogue with diverse cultures and religious traditions, and to serve the cause of reconciliation and peace. The books published reflect the views of their authors and do not represent the official position of the Maryknoll Society. To learn more about Orbis Books, please visit our website at www.orbisbooks.com.

Copyright © 2022 by Harry H. Singleton III
Published by Orbis Books, P.O. Box 302, Maryknoll, NY 10545-0302.
All rights reserved.
The Scripture quotations contained herein are from the New Revised Standard Version: Catholic Edition, Copyright © 1989 and 1993, by the Division of Christian Education of the National Council of the Churches of Christ in the United States of America. Used by permission. All rights reserved.
No part of this publication may be reproduced or transmitted in any form or by any means, electronic or mechanical, including photocopying, recording, or any information storage or retrieval system, without prior permission in writing from the publisher.
Queries regarding rights and permissions should be addressed to: Orbis Books, P.O. Box 302, Maryknoll, NY 10545-0302.
Manufactured in the United States of America

Library of Congress Cataloging-in-Publication Data

Names: Singleton III, Harry H., 1965- author.
Title: Forever in thy path : the God of black liberation / Harry H. Singleton.
Description: Maryknoll, New York : Orbis Books, [2022] | Includes bibliographical references and index. | Summary: "Makes the case that the eternal power of God's liberating presence will ultimately defeat the historical power of white supremacy"— Provided by publisher.
Identifiers: LCCN 2021035161 (print) | LCCN 2021035162 (ebook) | ISBN 9781626984707 (print) | ISBN 9781608339327 (ebook)
Subjects: LCSH: African Americans—Religion. | Blacks—Religion. | Black theology.
Classification: LCC BR563.B53 S56 2022 (print) | LCC BR563.B53 (ebook) |
DDC 200.89/96073—dc23
LC record available at https://lccn.loc.gov/2021035161
LC ebook record available at https://lccn.loc.gov/2021035162

In memory of
Reverend William P. Diggs
(1926–2020)

and

Presiding Elder Charles J. Graves
(1935–2020)

Stalwart pastors and humanitarians,
who have indelibly laid their hands on this theologian

God of our weary years,
God of our silent tears,
Thou who has brought us
thus far on the way;
Thou who has by Thy might
Led us into the light,
Keep us forever in the path
We pray. Amen.
—James Weldon Johnson, *Lift Ev'ry Voice*

Your word is like a lamp to my feet,
and a light for my path.
—Psalm 119:105 (NIV)

Contents

Acknowledgments	ix
Introduction	xi
The Negro's God	xi
The God of Black Liberation	xxvi
1 The Path of Freedom	1
Why a God of Black Liberation?	7
The Nature–History Challenge	14
The Accommodationism Challenge	19
God's Freedom and the New Covenant	25
2 The Path of Conversion	32
Conversion and Christian Freedom	34
Conversion Seeking Truth	39
Conversion, Preaching, and Militant Religion	45
Conversion and the Black Christ	50
3 The Path of Obedience	57
Christian Obedience in an Oppressed Context	60
Obedience to God and Human Liberation	67
Obedience, Black Liberation, and the Life of Jesus	74
4 The Path of Righteousness	81
The God of Social Righteousness	84
Divine Righteousness in a Racist Society	90
The Radical Demand of God's Love for the Oppressed	94
The Righteousness of God as the Wrath of God	101

5 The Path of Justice	108
God's Presence in the Stand for Justice	111
One God . . . Two Histories	118
God, Oppressive Laws, and Justice	123
Divine Justice and the Dispossessed	129
6 The Path of Liberation	135
The Spiritual Nature of the Liberation Struggle	139
The Sacred Nature of the Liberation Struggle	145
God and the Language of Liberation	152
Black Liberation and the Salvation of the World	158
7 The Path of Eternity	162
History as the Venue of the Coming Kingdom	167
The New Narrative of Death	173
Run Away and Get to the North	178
Index	183

Acknowledgments

Special thanks to the following persons and institutions: Benedict College for granting me a sabbatical in the fall of 2019 to begin research for what has now become this book; my former colleagues at Benedict College, whom I miss and who continue to sustain me with their dogged strength in acutely trying times; Dr. Valinda Littlefield, Professor of History at the University of South Carolina, who has had my proverbial back through the ebbs and flows of penning this work; Drs. Qiana Whitted, Director of the African American Studies Department, and Erin Roberts, Chair of the Religious Studies Department at the University of South Carolina, for their highly vested interest in my work; the staff of the University of South Carolina Library for its timely assistance in pointing me in the right direction for sources for this work and future works; Payne Theological Seminary in Wilberforce, Ohio, and longtime colleague Dr. Herbert Marbury for the gracious invitation to deliver two lectures on redemption and salvation in Black theology in early fall 2019, which provided a seamless transition into this work; and to my family, both nuclear and extended, who continue, along with God, to be my "shelter from a stormy blast."

Introduction

As we now have the eightieth anniversary of the 1938 publication of Benjamin E. Mays, *The Negro's God as Reflected in His Literature*, in our rearview mirror, we are indebted to Mays for the first landmark study on African Americans' diverse understandings of God. It still serves as the most comprehensive study on God in the history of Black people in this country. Mays's masterful work examines the different time periods in which Black people's understanding of God evolved: first from 1760 to 1865 (Emancipation); then from 1865 to 1914 (World War I); and finally from 1914 to 1938 (the publication of the book). From those three periods, Mays was able to identify four images of analysis: physical and emotional security; otherworldly/compensatory; atheistic; and social reconstruction. Let us now examine these different periods more closely.

The Negro's God

The first theme, *the belief in the God of physical and emotional security*, is understandable given that there was no sense of earthly remedy in the beginning and in the early stages of the slave trade. Kidnapped from Africa and brought to an unknown land, the new slaves had no earthly relationships with those who could provide avenues to emancipation. Furthermore, the hostility of slavery and the physical and emotional trauma associated with its subhuman condition—breaking up of families, naked public auctions, rapes, brandings, and merciless labor and whippings—lent itself to embracing a God who would provide some type of escape from the daily grind of inhuman labor and no recognition as human beings. Yet, even after emancipation and into post-Reconstruction, when the *Plessy v. Ferguson* Supreme Court decision of 1896 legally sanctioned racism once again, Black people felt a morbid sense of déjà vu in that they had no earthly outlets for social redress from white terror and so turned to the God of physical and emotional security. It was this God that Black people "fell back on" in the era of Jim Crow when public forms of racial humiliation such as lynchings, and the American government's legal approval of it, began to increase dramatically. Black people began to leverage God in spirited worship services and frequent prayers as a measure of relief from the daily indignities of legal separation and the often violent means by which whites maintained order in Dixie! Ultimately, for Mays, this approach to God and divine activity was a test of human will to endure slavery and segregation whereby Black people began to adjust themselves to thinking that racism was a permanent fixture in American life. Thus, Black people began to reason that this God was testing them to be obedient to their bondage not for a radical change in the racial demographic but for acceptance into heaven after death—a model of God, no doubt, taught to slaves by white pastors in plantation life!

Mays, however, found this model of God suspect inasmuch as it offered no freedom-seeking remedy for Black people in this world but ultimately showed its limitations by keeping Black people in a state of subordination, with God's apparent approval. His concern with this God was that it had no connection to the Black freedom struggle; and, therefore, God was still viewed as a condoner of white privilege, no matter the comfort brought to Black people through spirited worship services and frequent prayers. Mays writes,

> The belief that God is testing us out when trouble falls upon us thick and fast is one that makes it possible for us to bear the load without complaint. It is equally soothing and comfortable if one can believe that God is with him in the midst of his trouble. The person is less lonesome if he believes this. The idea seems to strengthen one to endure and to hold on

rather than to work to eliminate the source of irritation....
It gives one confidence but the idea adheres closely to traditional, compensatory patterns. It is a call to complacency and there is no effort at constructive rehabilitation of the idea of God in terms of social and economic adjustment.[1]

Importantly, Mays saw in this model of God a propensity on the part of Blacks to trust in God to make things better in the personal realm if they endured their collective troubles, that is, slavery. In this model, God is seen as the author of Black suffering who is demanding that Black people, as a test of faith, take on this suffering in order to receive blessings in the hereafter that will be incomparable to the current troubles experienced. This is exemplified in songs like "Trouble Don't Last Always" and "Didn't My Lord Deliver Daniel from the Lions' Den?" Here, deliverance is understood as an alleviation of one's temporary suffering in exchange for a heavenly blessing. In other words, faith in God means holding steadfast for an extraordinary blessing. The biblical character Job is often the model for this approach to God.

> The thing to do in a crisis like this is to be patient and trust God. If you trust God, he will multiply your riches and give peace and rest. This was the situation in Job's case and it is implied that what God did for Job, He will do now.[2]

Yet, for Mays, this image of God still lends itself to shortcomings. For not only does it call for Black people to suffer in the name of God, it keeps God's efficacy in personal fulfillment.

> The implication is that for one to get riches and prosperity is to trust God and never doubt or question his (God's) ways. If troubles are prerequisites for great blessings from God, they should be welcomed and they should be easy to bear. If troubles are sent by God incident to showers of blessings,

---

1. Benjamin E. Mays, *The Negro's God as Reflected in His Literature* (Westport, CT: Greenwood Publishing, 1969; orig., 1938), 190.
2. Mays, *The Negro's God*, 190.

one has no right to try and avoid them, and he (she) should be able to carry them with a smile and with comparative ease. The idea serves as an opiate for the people and it supports and tends to perpetuate the traditional, compensatory views so prevalent among the Negro masses.[3]

Thus, for Mays, the image of God as providing physical and emotional security is inauthentic in that it never considers the possibility of freedom in this world. Devoid of any physical and emotional security, Black people came to rely on a God who authored a highly emotionalized faith expression that has been more palliative than a call to freedom. In short, trying not to think about white racism by using religion as an escapist rather than a transformative phenomenon diminishes the impact of Christian experience on emancipation and keeps faith focused on personal concerns.

Mays's second model is that of *otherworldliness*, which has been implied by the first model. In Black literature, this is the model of God for which Mays has the least patience. To that point, Mays takes his place with most if not all freedom fighters in the Black prophetic radical tradition by exposing the connection between an otherworldly approach to God and white Christian teaching to Black people that God would accept them in heaven after death if, and only if, they were faithful servants to whites on earth, that is, did not subvert the slavocracy. In other words, the God of compensatory reward favors a kingdom devoid of Black freedom and considers human participation in bringing about freedom the highest sin. The compensatory God encourages waiting on God until the end time and maintains that human strivings for freedom betray God's wisdom. In so doing, passive toleration of injustice by the oppressed is understood as ideal Christian behavior. In short, the essence of religious experience is found in a "spiritual" clinging to God, not fighting for justice.

Here, Mays employs two terms to express "otherworldliness." The first term is *shallow pragmatism*—an image of God that is

---

3. Mays, *The Negro's God*, 191.

unrelated to racial injustice in this world. The pragmatic intervention of God still holds sway but is not an intervention that usurps historical realities of collective human suffering. Mays finds this approach unacceptable, especially given God's intervention in the Israelites' bondage in Egypt. Furthermore, this model not only condones total capitulation to whites as the epitome of what it means to be Black and Christian, but it offers no solution to Black suffering on earth; there is no hope or even belief that Black people should ever be free in this world. Rather, God's purpose is to provide fulfillment in other areas of human existence—healthy children, long life, limited illness, food, clothing, shelter of a reasonably good quality, and gratitude for creation but no fulfillment in social justice. He writes,

> The ideas are compensatory when used or developed to support a shallow pragmatism. That is, a belief or idea may be accredited as true if it satisfies our desire, "if it uplifts and consoles"; or if it makes us "happier to believe it," even though the belief or idea does not fit observed facts.[4]

For Mays, such an image of God was irrevocably compensatory in that it diverted Black people's attention away from collective suffering and ignored the "observed facts" of racism in all its manifold expressions. Those "observed facts" reveal the contradiction between freedom and enslavement that should drive any community's theological energies to rectifying that contradiction. Mays is clearly more inclined to a God who calls us to the task of ending racism as a primary concern rather than treating it as an ancillary concern.

The second term Mays uses to convey an otherworldly God is *negative goodness*. Mays recognizes that he is dealing with well-intentioned, sincere people engaged in an expression of faith that seeks to fulfill them and please God but ultimately runs itself to an impotent end in that it prolongs Black suffering rather than ends it. He is convinced that "ideas of God that are used to support an oth-

---

4. Mays, *The Negro's God*, 14.

erworldly view are ideas that adhere to traditional, compensatory patterns, those ideas that encourage one to believe that God is in heaven and is all right with the world, and finally, those that tend to produce a negative goodness in the individual based on a fear of the wrath of God here or in the next world,"[5] run counter to the God of the Bible. Based on this understanding of God, the wrath of God will be incurred for getting involved in any "subversive" behavior to end slavery. Mays saw this as the intent of white Christian leadership—to produce obedient slaves rather than militant slaves!

Mays saw this image of God present in the poetry of both Jupiter Hammon and Phyllis Wheatley. He was particularly repelled by Hammon's excessive dependence on the slaveholding community for the necessities of life and his contentment with slave life causing him to gladly relinquish freedom in this world. More disconcerting for Mays was Hammon's admonitions to slaves to frown on rebellion and think of their bondage as little as possible.

> Let me beg of you, my dear African brethren, to think very little of your bondage in this life; for your thinking of it will do no good. If God designs to set us free, he (God) will do it in his own time and way; but think of your bondage to sin and Satan, and do not rest until you are delivered from it.[6]

As for Wheatley, her renunciation of Africa's goodness and her joy at being enslaved served as a prime example to Mays of the impact that the pervasive nature of slavery and white Christian teaching to Blacks about Africa's "darkness" can and did have on Black self-image. This had in large part to do with Wheatley's good, even highly gratuitous, treatment by her masters in comparison to other masters, especially in their teaching her to read and write. Thus, Wheatley's writings reflected her particular existence and did not extend to the critical analysis of the toll slavery exacted on the psyche of Black people, nor did her writings render a larger theological valuation of an institution that treated other Blacks in a far

---

5. Mays, *The Negro's God*, 14–15.
6. Mays, *The Negro's God*, 99.

more ungodly way. In short, Mays would have liked to have seen Wheatley transcend her personal treatment and place the moral depravity of slavery itself at the forefront of her literary contribution. He notes,

> It seems that Phyllis Wheatley was equally thankful that God had brought her from ignorant and benighted Africa to enlightened, "civilized" America. Her attitude toward life and slavery, like Jupiter Hammon's, was greatly influenced by the kind treatment she received at the hands of the Wheatley's.... Hammon, therefore, could advise Negroes to obey their masters and Phyllis Wheatley could write almost ignoring the facts of slavery—certainly showing no progressive, militant attitude toward its abolition.[7]

In short, neither Hammon nor Wheatley views God in terms of social change. Consequently, Mays saw in this image a negative goodness in that it conveyed a well-meaning Christian commitment but had a negative impact on authentic Black progress.

The third image of God is what Mays calls the God of *atheism*, which he found in the theological literature of the Black community. This terminology, however, is not an accurate characterization. Mays does not imply that the literature affirms the literal nonexistence of God as is understood in Greek philosophical tradition, but, rather, it portrays a God who seemingly has no interest in the Black freedom movement.

Mays identifies the thought of AME Bishop Daniel Payne as a prime example of the "atheist" typology. A stalwart in the Black freedom struggle throughout his life, Payne publicly posed the question that many a Black person has surely pondered in private, and that is, whether God is as interested in Black suffering as God

---

7. Mays, *The Negro's God*, 104–105. Such a critique is not lost on contemporary discourse in the African American community regarding those who have ascended to the middle and upper classes and have no substantive worldview regarding institutional racism and its impact on less fortunate Black people!

was with Israelite suffering in the Exodus account. Payne became disillusioned with living life through a faith lens when the school he created in Charleston, South Carolina, in 1829 to educate slaves was abruptly shut down in 1835 by the South Carolina state legislature. That body ratified an anti-slavery teaching bill that fined, imprisoned, or administered fifty lashes to anyone, Black or white, who was caught teaching slaves how to read or write. The ratification led to Payne having to close the school, and from there to question the divine will. Payne questioned how a God who liberated the Israelites from Egyptian bondage could continue to allow a racist status quo to prosper when that God had come to be known as a liberator in the Black faith community. More particularly, how could God not end a lily-white political system that frames laws so diametrically opposite to God's will and so severely truncates the achievement of Black aspirations? Payne expresses his disappointment and then continues to leverage the power of God to act as a liberator in the future.

> Sometimes it seemed as though some wild beast had plunged his fangs into my heart, and was squeezing out its life-blood. Then I began to question the existence of God, and to say: "If he (God) does exist, is he (God) just? If so, why does he (God) suffer one race to oppress and enslave another, to rob them by unrighteous enactments of rights, which they hold most dear and sacred?" Sometimes I wished for the lawmakers what Nero wished—"that the Romans had but one neck." I would be the man to sever the head from its shoulders. Again said I: "Is there no God?" But then there came into my mind those solemn words: "With God one day is as a thousand years and a thousand years as one day. Trust in him (God), and he (God) will bring slavery and all its outrages to an end." These words from the spirit world acted on my troubled soul like water on a burning fire, and my aching heart was soothed and relieved from its burdens and woes.[8]

---

8. Bishop Daniel A. Payne, "Recollection of Seventy Years," in Mays, *The Negro's God*, 49.

What you see from Payne is more of a lapse in judgment about God's power as opposed to an outright disavowal of God. Also, you do not get from Payne the relinquishing of the struggle for freedom, as was the case with Wheatley and Hammon. What emerged was a reasonable questioning of God's "existence" in the face of such deadly racial violence and structural injustice, especially after the ratification of such a devastating piece of legislation by the South Carolina General Assembly. More important, Payne is firmly focused on the Black freedom struggle as his ministerial calling and is prepared to continue with that struggle, even if God is not enlisted as a copartner. In short, Payne's passion for justice led him to have unshakable faith in the realization of Black freedom with or without the help of God! His "trust in God" was not an invitation to human inactivity, as was the case with the compensatory model. His was an unburdening trust—more akin to an emptying of an evil spirit that sidetracked him from singular focus on the Black struggle for freedom than a complete break with seeing the world through the lens of a liberating divine presence. Consequently, the atheistic image has more to do with a lack of patience with God's seeming disinterest in Black freedom than a refutation of God's literal existence.

Connected with this image of God for Black people was the idea that God permits tragedies to occur as an expression of God's omnipotence. This dimension of God's "atheistic" leanings is seen most prominently in personal strivings and physical death, representing the morbid prospect of God permitting overwhelming difficulties over the course of a lifetime, and if that were not enough, then sending one to physical death. Mays references a sermon reflective of the time.

> If death comes to you, it comes because God permits it, and if God permits it, you ought to take a Christian view of the situation. If God permits it to come to you just say, "I am no better than anybody else." We ought not to set ourselves against God and say God has done injustice by us.[9]

---

9. Mays, *The Negro's God*, 71.

For Mays, his concern was that this image of God affirms too uncritically that every occurrence in the universe was an intentional product of the mind of God. This was and still is a staple part of orthodox Christian faith and is in large part the cornerstone of the white Christian establishment's argument that Black subordination/inferiority is at the behest of God. This idea of God adheres closely to traditional compensatory patterns, not only because it is expressive of orthodox Christianity and lessens the grief sustained by death but also because it has the tendency to lead one to take a complacent, laissez-faire attitude toward life in that the believer sees the will of God in all that happens.[10]

Mays's theological concern is justified. Christian tradition has been more interested in instilling a fear of God in its adherents for obedience to its directives with the assurance that a harmonious relationship with God will ensue and God will fulfill human desires. This is accomplished through the attribute of God's omnipresence lurking diligently to punish those who do not adhere to the divine will. The common denominator throughout the Christian tradition, unfortunately, is that Black suffering is not seen as sinful but rather as the key to salvation for both Black and white alike. More importantly, Mays discerns that we have inherited a Christian tradition in which the ultimate goal regarding freedom is a meek, mild, and disengaged Black community. This is why Black insurrection in plantation life was branded as sinful and still has a difficult time finding its place in constructive Christian discourse. Consequently, the atheistic model is not so much about God's existence/nonexistence as about one that is rooted in a dreaded fear of usurping the American status quo: white privilege, Black constraint, and the destiny of the religious individual.

> Though based on fear, the idea that God is everywhere and sees all that one does has a restraining influence upon conduct. It makes a difference in one's life for it promotes goodness that lacks positive action. This idea of God is also

---

10. Mays, *The Negro's God*, 72.

compensatory in its effect because its restraining influence is based on the traditional idea that God is to be feared and that the end sought is other-worldly.[11]

Certainly, that fear originates in the link that white Christian leadership placed between divinity and slavocracy with the understanding that for slaves to seek its demise was likely to incur God's wrath. Mays saw this coercive theological construction as the principal motivation for white Christian leadership exposing Blacks to Christianity. Thus, Mays discerned correctly that the will of God was leveraged in the legitimation of the slavocracy and, therefore, was removed from the equation of Black freedom. Mays "found Black people's extensive otherworldly/compensatory understanding of God in the early colonial spirituals, that is, they lead one to repudiate this world, consider it a temporary abode, and look to heaven for a complete realization of the needs and desires that are denied expression in this world."[12]

The fourth image of God is that of *social reconstruction*. This idea of God does not entertain human oppression in any form nor does this God allow religious faith to be used to legitimate Black suffering. This God does not create oppressive contexts but acts in history to destroy them. More importantly, this God sees Black freedom as the most pressing issue in human existence, not spirited worship services or a strong prayer life. In short, this idea of God, for Mays, inverts the God of Christian tradition and frees Black people to fight for freedom. Mays clearly wanted to direct the reader to the God of social reconstruction—the God who empowered Black people to change their condition and not simply use the names of God and Jesus to escape their suffering in a white racist world, no matter how satisfying that may have been on Sunday morning!

Given the history of Black oppression, Black people's walk with God has been therapeutic if not necessary. But for Mays, this God,

---

11. Mays, *The Negro's God*, 73.
12. Mays, *The Negro's God*, 72.

no matter how therapeutic, was more compensatory than socially engaged. Referencing his own upbringing in the church in Greenwood County, South Carolina, Mays explains,

> Long before I knew what it was all about, and since I learned to know, I heard the Pastor of the church of my youth plead with the members of his congregation not to try to avenge the wrongs they suffered, but to take their burdens to the Lord in prayer. Especially did he do this when the racial situation was tense or when Negroes went to him for advice concerning some wrong inflicted upon them by their oppressors. During these troublesome days, the drowning of Pharaoh and his host in the Red Sea, the deliverance of Daniel from the Lions' Den, and the protection given the Hebrew children in the Fiery Furnace were all pictured in dramatic fashion to show that God in due time would take things in hand. Almost invariably after assuring them that God would fix things up, he ended his sermon by assuring them further that God would reward them in Heaven for their patience and long-suffering on the earth. Members of the congregation screamed, shouted, and thanked God. The pent up emotions denied normal expression in everyday life found an outlet. They felt relieved and uplifted. They had been baptized with the "Holy Ghost." They had their faith in God renewed and they could stand it until the second Sunday in the next month when the experience of the previous second Sunday was duplicated. . . . This idea of God had telling effects upon Negroes in my home community. But it kept them submissive, humble, and obedient.[13]

Mays makes little secret for his partiality to the God of social reconstruction. The "realness" of God, for Mays, was not best understood as one who encouraged Black people to patiently endure their suffering until the end of human history or to take solace in a better world beyond this one.

Mays opted instead for the God of social reconstruction, identi-

---

13. Mays, *The Negro's God*, 26.

fying those approaches to ministry and leaders who saw resistance to white supremacy as the most viable appropriation of God for Black people. Even though the spirituals that reflected the compensatory model of God far outnumbered those that reflected the God of social reconstruction, their minority presence in the life of the church did not diminish their theological substance.

> Although the majority of the Spirituals are compensatory and other-worldly, it would be far from the truth to say that all of them are of that character. Even in the Spirituals the Negroes did not accept without protest the social ills which they suffered. "Go Down Moses," "Oh Freedom," and "No More, No More, No More Auction Block for Me" are illustrative of the Spirituals that revolt against earthly conditions without seeking relief from Heaven.[14]

In the light of the origins of Black suffering in slavery, Mays saw "Go Down Moses" as a contemporary fit for the Black condition and God's desire to see oppressed people go free in this world, thus contradicting models of God that teach an oppressed people that they have no hope of freedom in this world. But more galvanizing, Mays saw in "Oh Freedom" the true spirit of resistance to white racism and in the slaves' cry, "Oh Freedom o-ver me! an' befo' I'd be a slave, I'd be buried in my grave, an' go home to my Lord an' be free"—God's disdain with human bondage. Heaven then became not an escape from engagement with earthly oppression but an honorable destination for the martyr who dared challenge a racist status quo. Thus, heaven was given a liberating and not a compensatory meaning.

Sitting at the core of the God of social reconstruction is the affirmation of the equal worth of all human beings. The notion of valuing racial superiority as a supreme virtue while claiming to worship a God who is "no respecter of persons" is itself a sinful falling away of human relationships.

---

14. Mays, *The Negro's God*, 28.

> Has God who made the white man and the black left any accord declaring us a different species? Are we not sustained by the same power, supported by the same food, hurt by the same wounds, wounded by the same wrongs, pleased with the same delights, and propagated by the same means? And should we not then enjoy the same liberty, and be protected by the same laws?[15]

Not only have Black people not been protected by the same laws but, at every turn, white legislators have been working to establish an America of white privilege and Black subordination. They have enacted egalitarian laws only after protracted demonstrations by Black people in which many lost their livelihood and their lives. America's lawmakers, mainly white, male, and Christian, have not only sanctioned white privilege historically but also divinely, because American laws have been intrinsically connected to the God of Christian experience and thus legitimized racism both historically and theologically.

Making human oppression legal is not only confined to the United States. We only need to look at apartheid in South Africa, the Holocaust during the Second World War, and the caste system in India to appreciate how formidable human oppression becomes through legal status. Thus, the true adherent of the God of freedom is not only committed to challenging the legitimacy of oppressive laws but also sees the true meaning of discipleship as intimately connected to exposing the corruptness of these contexts globally. For Mays, this meant understanding God as being able to transform any context of human oppression, no matter the nuances. In that sense, the God of social reconstruction calls us to the world of broken relationships and is therefore not given over to ascetic flights from the suffering of this world but compels us to leave the comfortable confines of the contemplative life and seek the redemption of humankind in the blood shed, symbolically or in reality, in the fight for freedom.

---

15. Words of abolitionist James Forten in Carter G. Woodson's, *Negro Orators and Their Orations*. Taken from Mays, *The Negro's God*, 112.

For Mays, the yearning for freedom is a gift from God based on the affirmation that the image of God resides in all human beings, including Black human beings! Consequently, we also reside in God. There is divine value in every human life, and every recipient is under obligation to God to respect that value, for all human life is precious unto God.[16] In other words, human longing for freedom is essential to the core of God's creation, and humans are required not to subvert that creative plan but to realize it through the reflection of the divine within.

> God and humanity are one. God has set no geographical boundaries nor racial limitations. There is no divine right of race. The rights of humanity are divine and they cannot be divested by reason of race. We are all God's creatures. God has created the Negro in His own image. He has made no superior races and no inferior races.[17]

In short, the Negro is God's most perfect handiwork. The human family is united in God. The Negro is on a special errand for God.... He is on the side of right, actively engaged in the struggle, but in cooperation with humanity.[18] Mays affirms a God who not only imbues Blacks with the ability to make right what whites have made wrong, but demands it in every oppressive context where undeserved human privilege and undeserved human suffering are in traumatic and violent relationship with each other. In such a context, God is the virtual balm in Gilead who can cure a racist heart of its evil and cure a passive heart of its fear. God has put the Negro and the white man in America to prove to the world that two races varying in culture and color can live together, each contributing to the welfare of the other.[19] For Mays, God is using this opportunity of racial strife as a proving ground to demonstrate God's majesty in realizing the kingdom, which is the full reconciliation of the Black

---

16. Mays, *The Negro's God*, 248.
17. Mays, *The Negro's God*, 250.
18. Mays, *The Negro's God*, 250.
19. Mays, *The Negro's God*, 250.

and white races. Mays is not engaged in a pipe dream but in realizing a world where the lamb and lion truly lie down together and share the resources of the earth equally. For this to happen, racist hearts must continue to be the spiritual target for Black people. At the same time, Mays was clear that Blacks must also exorcise white demons that have spawned a distorted adoration for white culture and aesthetics and an existential fear of the white power structure. This distorted adoration for whites is an invitation, a clarion call from God, for Black people to love what God had made them culturally and aesthetically! It is the God who demands that Black people sing with James Brown, "Say It Loud; I'm Black and I'm Proud."

In this sense, Mays was a *pre-liberation theologian*. He envisioned a faith that sees an intimate relationship between the God of the Bible and the freedom of the despised prior to the emergence of liberation as a school of theology. Even though he uses the term "social reconstruction," he uses it before it became known in theological circles as liberation theology. This is clear in *The Negro's God*, where Mays is critical of ideas of God that are compensatory/otherworldly, and yet he affirms ideas of God whose essence is expressed in the struggle for socio-political liberation. In close connection, he is also fond of the term "militant religion," or religious faith that inspires aggressive resistance, not docility, to white privilege.

The God of Black Liberation

Now that we hve taken an in-depth look at Mays's analysis of African Americans' experience of God, the reader is entitled to know its connection to this work. This book seeks to pick up where Mays left off—not with Mays's commitment to objectively demonstrating African Americans' diverse understandings of God (where death still disproportionately visits Black people, who has time for objectivity?) but with his clear partiality to the God of social reconstruction—a God who calls the faithful to militant religion . . . to societal reconstruction out of its bigoted ways. That God is more aptly referred to today as *the God of Black liberation*. This is the God who has taken Black people from slave quarters to the White House—the God who not only revealed that we are somebody despite white pronouncements to the contrary, but also the God who has been a transformative presence from the holds of the first ships, to the auction blocks, to the whipping posts, to the lynching tree, to the prison industrial complex, to the ghettos, to crumbling schools, and to staring down the gun of a white police officer. Present in each of these confrontations has been the God of Black liberation standing with strong Black men and women, instilling in them a courage "not given by this world," and, therefore, not able to be "taken by this world"—a God who demands that the world no longer operate the white way but the liberated way! Because this God has committed to transforming the context of oppressed Blacks in our time as God has done for the oppressed in previous contexts, James Cone proclaimed, "that it is not only appropriate but necessary to begin the doctrine of God with the insistence on his blackness."[20] This proclamation is not intended to isolate other races. It is, rather, an affirmation of the faith of a community that has had to encounter God in the bowels of white hostility. The God of Black liberation identifies with that hostility, given that Black suffering emerges out of one major crucible—blackness! God, therefore, makes the ultimate identification with blackness as a badge of shame historically as a basis for forging a decisive response to that shame. Thus, the freedom of Black people *becomes not just a historical issue but a salvific issue*—an issue of ultimate concern for God. As Major Jones writes,

> The task of conceiving God's reality has visited the Black religious community by a different route than it took to the White counterpart. Nevertheless, that problem has come. The shape of this visitation concerns what God is doing in the world today, and how God is involved in the liberation, freedom, and ultimate salvation of Black people....

---

20. James H. Cone, *A Black Theology of Liberation* (New York: Orbis Books, 1990), 121. First published in 1970.

The reality of God bears directly on questions of the earthly struggle for liberation.[21]

Like the Israelites who were led out of slavery in Egypt, the God of Black liberation has led Black people out of institutionalized slavery and segregation. Most importantly, this God has sent messengers like Moses to the Israelites to inform the world that Black people are not slaves by nature (Aristotle) nor does the God of Jesus Christ ordain their subordination to whites as a natural order (white Christianity) but that Black humanity is a direct reflection of the *imago dei*, despite white Christian proclamations to the contrary. Whether it was Frederick Douglass running north to freedom or Harriet Tubman leading thousands to freedom on the Underground Railroad or demonstrators staring down tear gas, water hoses, dogs, billy clubs in peaceful public protests demanding constitutionally what should have already been theirs, the God of Black liberation has been an ever-present mainstay in the abyss of white trauma. For Black people, that mainstay hinges on the promise that "I am with you always, to the end of the age" (Matt 28:20). It is that God, the God of Black liberation, who, according to Mays, has brought Black people to this day—still with crucial struggles ahead but ever more empowered by the giant examples of courage that have preceded them!

When the God of Black liberation lodges in the heart, what seems to be impossible suddenly becomes pregnant with the hope of freedom. While the fears of economic reprisal and even death are well founded, given what the white power structure has perpetrated on Black people and what it has done to weaken Black leadership, what God gives in Jesus—the gift of eternal life—removes fear in the oppressed, and transhistorical faith removes historical fear. Given that we have come this far by faith, a faith "the size of a mustard seed" that has moved the mountain of white supremacy and will prove in the end to be its ultimate nemesis,

---

21. Major J. Jones, *The Color of God: The Concept of God in Afro-American Thought* (Macon, GA: Mercer University Press, 1987), 24.

the cries of "move" will continue to resonate throughout America and the world without fear, and the intellectual, aesthetic, and cultural denunciations of Black humanity will cease, and all barriers preventing the full participation of Black people as equal human beings in society will come down. This is the meaning of Black liberation! This must be the meaning of divine essence for our time!

It is to the God of Black liberation, the God that James Weldon Johnson describes in the last verse of the Negro national anthem, "Lift Ev'ry Voice," as "The God of our weary years, / the God of our silent tears, / the God who has brought us thus far on the way, / thou who has by thy might led us into the light, / keep us *forever in thy path* we pray," to which we have pledged our eternal allegiance. That light has been the fulfillment of hope in a hopeless world . . . of hope in a world of physical and mental devastation, a light that has been the fulfillment of divine presence as a liberator in a nation where white privilege is pervasive, and a light that has been the fulfillment of conquering enemies, turning them into "footstools." It is an eternal light that has illumined our path from slavery and beyond, and it is a path in which the psalmist proudly proclaimed, "your word is a lamp to my feet, and a light for my path" (Ps 119:105).

This work elaborates further on the meaning of that path that God has created and illuminated in our darkest moments in this American sojourn. A path constantly forged by the God of Black liberation in the spiritual DNA of Black people that compels them to resist encroachments on their humanity, to not let any racist "turn us around," and to "keep on walking, keep on talking, marching up to freedom land." A path of several dimensions, seven of which will be our focus—freedom, conversion, submission, righteousness, justice, liberation, and eternity—and which have proved indispensable in our quest for human liberation.

1

The Path of Freedom

The path of freedom undergirds and informs all other paths in that it is the foundation of the universe because creation itself is an act of freedom. It undergirds all other paths in that it is God's central concern in contexts of human oppression. It informs all other paths in the sense that freedom is the essence of divine being. Thus, when God created the heavens and the earth it was a free act and not one of necessity. The world necessarily emerges out of freedom from a God who is neither bound by the world nor needs it for existence. As Nikolai Berdyaev wrote,

> Man is subordinated to the universal unity in relation to which God is fully immanent. But God is also completely transcendent in relation to this universal unity and to the process which takes place in it. And this transcendence of God, the freedom of God from world necessity, and from all objectivity, is the source of the freedom of man, it constitutes the very possibility of the existence of personality.[1]

In other words, the creative order is such that the relationship between God and humanity is anything but mutually dependent. While we are dependent on God for life, God is in no way dependent on human existence or personality for existence or sustenance. This is why God is referred to by the scientific community

---

1. Nikolai Berdyaev, *Slavery and Freedom* (New York: Charles Scribner's Sons, 1944), 70.

as the First Cause, or that which caused the universe to come into existence. As such, God could have existed without a universe and all life forms that exist in that universe. This is the meaning of the contingent being of all life forms, that is, dependent on a being not of its essential makeup to create them. The means that living beings *are the creation of a free God and as such are created inescapably in freedom.*

In this sense, humans were created in freedom and to express that freedom as part of the cosmological DNA of the world in service to the one who created us in that same freedom. Thus, beyond physical makeup, we are free as creations of a free God. We are created as one human family, and the possibilities lie in free will relative to human decisions that demonstrate that free will—both in resonance with divine will and/or without that will. In Christian anthropology, we witness such free will early on with Adam and Eve. The gift from God to make free decisions became readily apparent in direct disobedience. On the one hand, it is clear that humans have a broader capacity of freedom than objects in the universe such as the sun, moon, stars, and so on, which are regulatory in function. It is also clear that humans have a broader capacity of freedom than other life forms, which tend to be more animalistic in function. On the other hand, it is clear that humans have the freedom to control the vital affairs of the world through acts that can either reflect God's essence or reject God's essence. Dorothee Sölle explains further:

> Christian belief in creation relates to the creature and its independent existence; it is made free. Adam and Eve are free to eat the apple; they are not compelled by destiny; they do not stand under an absolute necessity. According to Jewish-Christian tradition, *human beings are always understood in terms of freedom.* And freedom also means capable of evil.[2]

By evil, Sölle is referring to human acts that reject God's essence.

---

2. Dorothee Sölle, *Thinking About God: An Introduction to Theology* (Philadelphia: Trinity Press International, 1990), 44.

What makes human decision even more complicated is that what is considered good or evil is itself subject to human creation in freedom. In other words, the construction of moral and ethical frameworks for judging human behavior are also made by the same human beings who commit the acts. Thus, in the unfolding of Adam and Eve's narrative, they were given a single directive and disobeyed, but contemporary moral frameworks take into consideration a much broader scope of human decisions. Whether it be through a family, a nation's laws, or a religious community, valuations of human behavior are not as clear, particularly when they are connected to divine command. In addition, those behaviors may be deemed "good" by one community but deemed evil in another community based on that community's understanding of God. Nowhere has this been more true than in the formation of slavery and other forms of systemic human denial of one group of humans over another when religious institutions have maintained that that enslavement and/or systemic denial are *expressions of obedience to God* (see chap. 3). The destruction of such systems becomes much more formidable given their connection to divine obedience. In one sense, seeking an end to systemic oppression demonstrates the desire for the slave class to return the human family to the freedom with which God created us, but in another sense it brings out the master class's dogged proclivity to maintain its privilege, even if it means the commodification of other humans. Thus, over several generations, the internalization of such frameworks becomes normative for those of the master class, and the members of the slave class find that normativity the juggernaut of its existence. The slave class, in turn, seeks to bring an end to their suffering in obedience to God as well. Thus, the unfolding of Adam and Eve's narrative has taken us from a decision about fruit to living obediently in God in a master–slave context.

Not surprising, the master–slave division has led to the formation of two different moral frameworks and two different views of God. While historically the master class holds that God has condoned "masterdom," the slave class holds that God has not. On the one hand, the master class has constructed a "theology" that legitimates the master–slave division—and no less in the name of God. And that legitimation becomes the cornerstone of the master class's "civilization," with the slaves' fate given no liberating significance in the theological process. Religious expression becomes conveniently tied to rituals and personal morality that take freedom for the enslaved class out of the religious equation. On the other hand, the slave class has also developed a theology that takes straight aim at the master class's hypocrisy in seeking to maintain a sinful relationship at God's behest. For them, Jesus's rejection of this approach to the religious life is clearly evident. As Gutiérrez notes,

> "I never know you; depart from me" is a classical formula of the Bible for a complete and unconditional rejection. "On that day" those rejected will be termed "evildoers" because they did not feed the hungry or give drink to the thirsty (Matthew 25:31–45). The actions that such people claim as religious (prophesying, expelling demons, working miracles) were simply ritual gestures empty of concrete love for the poor brothers and sisters; therefore, God was not in these actions.[3]

Rather than equating God's freedom with the freedom of slaves, the master class validates its existence by making God's eternity synonymous with the eternity of existence of slavery and, in the ultimate rebuke of God, offers the slave class no chance of freedom "this side of Jordan." In so doing, the master class's theological perspective becomes the negation of itself by putting forward the validity of a master–slave relationship rather than a theology of human freedom. Thus, religion that emerges from master–slave theology is in a constant identity crisis for, like Pharaoh, it becomes a "hardened heart" religion affirming a civilization of excessive earthly privilege derived from "masterdom." Yet in light of that

---

3. Gustavo Gutiérrez, *The God of Life* (Maryknoll, NY: Orbis Books, 1991), 74.

privilege and the ideological way in which it is maintained, that is, manipulating the transcendence of God to condone or have no interest in the master–slave relationship, the master class stays in the path of God's chastisement.

> Transcendence can also be understood in a servile way and may mean the degradation of man. Transcendence can be interpreted as objectivization and exteriorization, and relation to it not as an inward act as transcension in freedom, but as the relation of slave to master. The way of liberation lies on the other side of traditional immanence and transcendence.[4]

In other words, the quest for liberation, once unnecessary to human history, becomes necessary, given that freedom has been severely compromised through the creation of a master-and-slave division. It also means that God now assumes the mode of liberator, championing the cause of the slave community. How could it be otherwise? As we have come to know the freedom of God through creation, we have also come to know the freedom of God through biblical revelation—a God who intervenes in oppressive relationships to restore them to the freedom that is God's essence. Thus, the master–slave relationship is a relationship alien to God's nature, which in turn makes the destruction of that relationship God's principal concern. Since God is interested in the true reflection of God's creative prerogative, God makes clear that the divine will is inextricably linked with the slaves, the voiceless, the dispossessed, the disinherited, the oppressed—those who have been systematically ostracized from full participation in society and therefore live out of their created essence. So long as there is an oppressed class, the human family will always be antithetical to God's created order—both slave *and* master. As Sölle reminds us,

> The various trends of liberation theology are agreed that the existing world order is hostile to creation, indeed that in its various forms of oppression by class rule, racism, sexism, and

---

4. Berdyaev, *Slavery and Freedom*, 70.

imperialism over nature it represents an attack on creation. The poor are deprived of their being created in the image of God.[5]

No God who creates in freedom can rest easy with a world rooted in a master–slave dynamic. God's creation has been compromised by the master's decision to make himself master and to use God's name to legitimate the creation of the slave. When those relationships emerge, God's cause becomes their destruction, for life and life more abundantly becomes death and death more abundantly through multiple generations of social, economic, political, and religious exploitation. God's disdain for those relationships becomes the path to which we commit ourselves not to a faith that serves the interests of the master but to a faith that serves the interests of the slave—a faith that champions freedom as a way of life, *the* way of life, as God inaugurates the return journey to freedom.

> Man is not searching for being but for truth and the meaning of existence. And man is confronted not by abstract truth but by The Truth, as the way and the life. "I am the Truth, the Way, and the Life."[6]

We know God's commitment because we saw it in Jesus. Word no longer remained word but became flesh as a direct identification with the urgency of the human return to freedom. Jesus's primary concern with freedom for the oppressed is a prominent theme in the Gospel of Luke. Commitment to human freedom is witnessed in Jesus's proclamation that he came to set at liberty those who are oppressed (Luke 4:18–19) and in the story of the good Samaritan (Luke 10:25–37). The former passage places the ministry of Jesus squarely in the struggle of the disinherited for freedom, while the latter one identifies Jesus's favor toward the Samaritans—those despised and stereotyped by the master class.

---

5. Sölle, *Thinking About God*, 49.
6. Berdyaev, *Slavery and Freedom*, 81.

> The poor (Greek *ptochoi;* the same word is used in Isaiah 61:1 LXX) in Luke are clearly those who lack the necessities of life. . . . It is to these that deliverance is proclaimed . . . the good news preached to them is given concrete form in the three statements that follow: release for captives; sight for the blind; and freedom for the oppressed. In all these instances we find one and the same proclamation, the dominant idea being *freedom*.[7]

Hence, Luke leaves no doubt about God's unqualified identification with the voiceless and their struggle for freedom.

Why a God of Black Liberation?

We have established that God's freedom in creation should also be reflected in society. Yet that has not been the case in modern history, particularly with the Black–white encounter in America. In fact, the paragon of human oppression in our time has been white racism in America. It is the personification of a world that is out of sync with God's creation. A God, whose nature is freedom, has witnessed the worst forms of physical and psychical abuse in modern history. But more tragically, God's name has been used to legitimate that abuse of people, mostly Black. But given the good news of God's historical intervention in oppressive relationships, and given that Black skin has come to symbolize oppressed humanity in our time, God's synchronous identification with that symbol, "blackness," transforms God into the God of Black liberation who takes on, as God's own, the struggle of Black people. The Christ event's meaning in our time is that God is at work in the Black community as it seeks to affirm its humanity in a society committed to Black suffering. It is the God of Black liberation who instills in Black people the necessary resolve, which is as eternal as God, to relentlessly fight for freedom; to restore the freedom with which God created the world. Thus, the freedom with which God created

---

7. Gutiérrez, *The God of Life*, 8.

the world is the basis on which Black people have been able to sustain their struggle for full human emancipation despite white attempts to discourage and destroy the hopes of Black people for a brighter day. In that sense, Black people, unable to place any trust in whites to guide them to freedom, have had to depend on another source—and one greater than white supremacy—a free and liberating God!

In biblical revelation, God's intervening power is always on the side of the slave and not on the side of the master. Thus, it follows that the God of the Bible, the God of Jesus Christ, is also the God of Black liberation.

> The revolutionary attitude of Black Theology stems not only from the need of black people to defend themselves in the presence of white oppression but also from its identity with biblical theology. Like biblical theology, it affirms the absolute sovereignty of God over his creation. This means that ultimate allegiance belongs only to God. Thus black people must be taught not to be disturbed about revolution or civil disobedience if the law violates God's purpose for man. The Christian man is obligated by a freedom grounded in the creator to break all laws that contradict human dignity.[8]

In essence, Cone is making the case that the freedom God gives in creation is also the freedom God gives in revolutionary movements to the abused and humiliated. This is why regardless of the proscriptions placed on the humanity of Black people by the white power structure, the militant response from Black people is a justifiable response in an unfree society and is a direct reflection of God's rage against Black oppression. Thus the uncompromising stand taken by Black people on the path of freedom does not come from unenlightened heathens who have no sense of human decency or from those trying to "stir the pot" of a postracial nation

---

8. James H. Cone, *Black Theology & Black Power* (Maryknoll, NY: Orbis Books, 1989), 137.

but is an inescapably passionate response to a racist society that is diametrically opposed to the God of Black liberation.

The God of Black liberation is opposed to any action that desecrates the *imago dei,* the image of God. For to do so is to deny freedom to fellow humans and to deny God.

> When man denies his freedom and the freedom of others, he also denies God. To be for God by responding creatively to the *imago dei* means that man cannot allow others to make him an It. It is this fact that makes black rebellion human and religious. When black people affirm their freedom in God they know that they cannot obey laws of oppression. By disobeying, they not only say Yes to God but also to their own humanity and the humanity of the white oppressor.[9]

In other words, Black people have chosen God and not whiteness. By saying "no" to white supremacy, Black people are actually acknowledging their common humanity with whites but are also acknowledging that because the spirit of freedom that lives in them comes from God they *can never accept a future as an oppressed people.* This is why the racial interaction between white and Black people for the soul of America has been so volatile. The two races have been in a historical tug of war seeking either the perpetuation of racial caste or a new America and world rooted in freedom. Whites have shown that they will and have done anything to maintain racial caste, from killing to lynching to rape to structural denial; to job, education, and housing discrimination; to tokenism; to stereotyping; and to criminal injustice. Yet all attempts have failed ultimately to carry out the desired result—destroy the will to racial justice in Black people! No amount of intellectual gamesmanship, violence, or unjust laws have been able to force Black people to accept second-class citizenship.

While there is a public recognition that this is currently a "white man's world," that recognition on the part of Black people has

---

9. Cone, *Black Theology & Black Power,* 137–38.

always been a current, and certainly not a future, concession. This is because the Black struggle for liberation is not merely a human struggle. From the time that the first boat carried the first West African on the Middle Passage, the struggle to free Black people has been taken up by the God of creation—the God of freedom. For in the makeup of human beings is the Spirit of God, who will not allow them to accept bondage because of the insatiable desire instilled in them by God to be the free creatures God intended them to be. It is indeed the *imago dei* that compels Black people to fight for their humanity, for in that expression God is not only an active participant but the God who instilled in them the same freedom that is the essence of divine being. Thus, the God whom Black people came to know was a God very different from the pseudo-God created by white Christian leaders to justify racism.

> The ideas of God are developed along the lines of social reconstruction in two particulars: the author [Reverend Nathaniel Paul] uses God to prove that slavery should and will be overthrown and he develops the idea to instill race pride and group self-respect in the Negro. The Negro therefore has no right to sit complacently by and accept slavery as God ordained; he has no reason to believe that he is inferior to other people.[10]

Thus, what gives the Black struggle for freedom its essentially *human* character is God's declaration of the inherent equal worth of all humans. What gives the Black struggle for freedom its essentially *religious* character is God's creation in freedom, which governs the universe. In this respect, Mays quotes Joseph M. Carr:

> Then let me ask the important question, Why! O Why! should not the coloured American citizen be equal, in all the qualities of the heart, and the powers of the mind, with his white brother? Has nature made him inferior? Has his great

---

10. Benjamin E. Mays, *The Negro's God as Reflected in His Literature* (Westport, CT: Greenwood Publishing, 1969; orig., 1938), 44.

Creator designed him to be, in any respect? Has he at any time, or on any occasion, declared it? Can there be a prophet produced, a revelation quoted, an oracle consulted, to unfold such an idea, to resolve such a problem, or expound such a theory? Ask the standard of truth, let Heaven's own inspiration be heard, and God himself speak! "All souls are mine," is his express declaration, "for my ways are equal," saith the Lord God, "and consequently all my works are founded on the same basis."[11]

The God of Black liberation makes clear that partisanship with the oppressed is a complete commitment. The God of Black liberation also makes clear that the theological sophistry that white Christian leadership has used to "prove" its superiority is rooted more in the will to power than in the power of God. Human favor belongs not only to whites but to all humans, and the complexion of skin does not make God more partial to one group over another. However, if biblical revelation is true to its narrative, then in contexts of oppression, God does make an unqualified identification with the oppressed and makes them God's chosen people. That is because God created the world in freedom, and it is to that freedom that we come to know how God acts in human history—the God of freedom acts on the side of the oppressed and that God also places in the oppressed the eternal desire to pursue freedom.

To say "no" to white supremacy but "yes" to God has indeed put Black people in the throes of every practical decision regarding race. But because Black people have come this far by faith and faith alone, ultimately, the decision has been for God and against white supremacy. It has literally meant the decision to be free and not slaves—to serve God and not mammon! And in so doing, the decision *for* God is a decision by the Black community to walk by faith and not by sight—the human longing for deliverance under the whip of white rule. More importantly, the decision to walk with God has also been a divine imperative. For the divine decision had

---

11. Mays, *The Negro's God*, 45.

been made when God heard the cries of Black people in the holds of ships, on the auction blocks, and in the anguish of mothers as newborns were snatched from their loins and sent to other plantations, while white infants were nursed to strength by those same Black women's breasts! It was then that God decided that Black people would be God's people, as the children of Israel were in biblical history. Thy kingdom had come; thy will had been done; Pharaoh's army had drowned in the Red Sea. As David Walker so eloquently expresses,

> God suffers some to go on until they are ruined forever!!! Will it be the case with the whites of the United States of America? We hope not—we would not wish to see them destroyed notwithstanding, they have and do now treat us more cruel than any other people have treated another, on this earth since it came from the hands of its Creator.... The will of God must however, in spite of us, *be done*.[12]

Walker lays out God's imperative for Black freedom and the consequence for whites for extending Black oppression. It also means Black people not accepting second-class citizenship and taking whatever shots at their disposal to deliver a blow to white racism. James Cone is right, "there are no assets to slavery." But furthermore, there are no assets to segregation; there are no assets to political injustice; there are no assets to passive resignation to white racism; and there are no assets to postracialism! Black Lives Matter because Black lives matter to God, not as murder victims given little or no justice because of their blackness and certainly not as inferiors ingratiating themselves with the white power structure for a token position but as wise creations that were made for freedom not bondage.

> Black people know who they are; and to know who you are is to set limits on your own being. It means that any act of

---

12. David Walker, *The Appeal to the Coloured Citizens of the World* (Baltimore, MD: Black Classic Press, 1993; orig., 1830), 61.

oppression will be met with an almighty Halt! Any act of freedom will be met with an almighty Advance![13]

The limits of freedom to which Cone refers do not mean a limit on Black people's freedom, which is no freedom at all. Rather, the limited structure represents the narrowly constructed decisions—the *path*—that God demands all humans make about taking one's rightful place along the path of freedom. The future of God's reign is clear: only by saying "no" to racial bigotry and "yes" to Black liberation will the freedom with which God created the universe be realized in history.

The God of Black liberation is on the scene today with an uncompromising message for both whites, who perpetuate racial caste, and Blacks, who perpetuate escapism—thy will be done! Regardless of the vicissitudes of history and the darkest moments in the trek from oppression to liberation, the God of Black liberation has been at the forefront of the Black struggle, leading Black people to the freedom that is God's essence. This is why Black people have been able to endure demonic treatment and respond in the way of freedom for they know that even if the particular act or movement is defeated in the historical moment, their efforts put one more chink in the armor of white privilege and signal the coming reign of God's liberating presence. As Major Jones states,

> Divine freedom—the very meaning of faith—is an Afro-Americanized God's presence in Black people's existence whereby they are given a new life that resides in a concept of God constantly being renewed. Even in the midst of bondage and defeat, Black people have always been able to celebrate, not bondage or defeat, but rather, human existence in spite of dehumanizing external bondage and the infernal exile of civil rights' defeats.[14]

---

13. Cone, *Black Theology & Black Power*, 141–42.
14. Major J. Jones, *The Color of God: The Concept of God in Afro-American Thought* (Macon, GA: Mercer University Press, 1987), 37.

Divine freedom means that, despite the pain of the existential moment, there is an eternal connectedness between the freedom for which Black people strive and the freedom that God gives in the covenant relationship with oppressed peoples. In other words, the pursuit of freedom is not just a human undertaking by oppressed communities, for the origin of their thirst for freedom is not human but divine!

The Nature–History Challenge

Black people, like all humans, were created in the image of God and are therefore free *in nature*.[15] But history presents another story. Black people have been anything but free. We still live in a nation where white males continue to make the major decisions, hold the major positions of power, and control its wealth. And the fact that white Christian leadership has developed a "substantive" Christian theology that proclaimed God's blessing on that deprivation of freedom has fortified white thinking that its treatment of Black people has not been evil but redemptive for both races. While the Black response has been consistent, the best pathway to bridging that nature–history incompatibility has never been uniform in strategy. But when Malcolm X maintained in his famous speech "The Ballot or the Bullet" that "I am not for separation and you're not for integration. What you and I are for is freedom," he was speaking to a singular goal in two dimensions of the struggle.

First, Malcolm was addressing the two most prominent methodologies in the struggle for Black freedom: integration and separation. Integration was the method favored by the civil rights movement. It sees America and whites as essentially good, and through moral suasion, whites can be convinced to see Black people as their equals and have American and global life reflect that

---

15. On the classic attempts to resolve this incompatibility between nature and human relationships, see Reinhold Niebuhr, *The Nature and Destiny of Man (Humanity)*, 2 vols. (New York: Charles Scribner's Sons, 1964; orig., 1941). See also Sölle, *Thinking About God*.

idea. In this sense, the civil rights community was of the opinion that the lion and the lamb could lie down together and become a paragon of national peace and harmony for the world. The civil rights movement saw the racial struggle as multigenerational and America's resources as the gateway to a more productive quality of life for future generations of Black people. In sum, the civil rights community saw the sharing of the nation's resources as the end goal of humans once at odds with each other racially and now living as constitutional protocol demanded. Thus, civil rights organizations saw as impractical the separatist methodology of Black nationalist groups, viewing them ultimately as Black supremacist groups that advocate replacing one form of racial supremacy with another. This seemed the logical conclusion to be drawn given the civil rights community's view of both whites and God. That is, whites were seen as good by nature and capable of repentance despite their treatment of Black people and their continual claims of racial superiority. The civil rights movement understood the divine as a co-partner, struggling with the Black community in its fight to throw off the shackles of white oppression and "convert" white people to a new morality regarding its treatment of Black people.[16]

Malcolm X, as a member of the Nation of Islam until the last couple of years of his life, saw separation as the best possible solution to the division between the races. In this view, Black people should be nationalists and seek to control the politics, economics, and cultural expression of their community. Black nationalists advocate a huge distrust of whites and are merciless in their criticism of the treatment of Black people by whites. Black nationalist organizations call for a separate nation state for Black people somewhere within the continental United States or in one of the Caribbean nations or West Africa, financed by the United States government since the two races will never have a congenial relationship. The

---

16. This view of Black freedom holds to the biblical theme of God's creation of all humans out of one blood and that to war against a fellow human is to war against oneself (see Mal 2:10).

lion will never lie down with the lamb, and there will be no sentimental or nonviolent peaceful solution to the race problem. Freedom will come only through physical distance between the two races whereby Black people will no longer be subject to the daily encroachments on their humanity by white people. This approach has much to do with a sobering assessment of America's highly unstable and violent racial history.

What has undergirded the Black nationalist philosophy is its view of whites and God. For Black nationalists, whites have no redeeming qualities and are too deeply entrenched in centuries of racist socialization to change their ways, and therefore, a true and lasting freedom for Black people is not attainable. God is seen not as co-partnering on the journey from slavery to freedom but rather as taking on an apocalyptic role. In other words, God is the one who will bring about Black liberation through God's destruction of the white race and returning Black people to the freedom in which they lived prior to the European conquests.[17]

Although both approaches—integration and separation—leave very little middle ground, and their leaders are passionate defenders of each methodology's singular effectiveness, they are, however, commonly united around two questions: How is white humanity to be judged and how is God to be "employed" in the process of moving from bondage to freedom? In short, both approaches espouse faith in God even as methodological disagreements abound. While the ideologies differ, the valuation of white actions and the continual quest for freedom do not. In other words, what is operative in both approaches is the interconnectedness between freedom and God, and more importantly, the understanding that the freedom of Black people is not to be compromised. In other words, *the goal of freedom* is made clear in both methodologies. Both methodologies are consistent in their

---

17. This view of Black freedom holds to the climactic end of the Israelite journey and the destruction of the Egyptian army with the Israelites crossing over the Red Sea on "dry ground" while Pharaoh's army was drowned (and killed!) in that same sea (see Exodus 14).

uncompromising call for a full, rather than a piecemeal, freedom for Black people.

Also operative in both approaches is the unquestioned trust in God to realize freedom. While one approach sees God as a co-struggling partner and the other as a destroyer of unrighteous whites, God's omnipotent and liberating presence is common in both. Given the interpretative nature of a nation's history, in this case its racial history, it is understandable that without an absolute knowledge of God, there would be ideological differences between Black people as to the most effective path to freedom. Yet there is very little disagreement that God is integral to that path.

The second aspect Malcolm was addressing in this statement is the idea of freedom: "What you and I are for is freedom." How could a people who had known only bondage for over three hundred years and been cut off from their precolonial days in Africa know what freedom is, let alone yearn for it, even at the cost of life? From whence would a people develop that yearning, or did it ever have to be developed? Whereas there are ideological differences in history, there are none in nature. Given that the ultimate agent of freedom created the universe, the foundation of the universe's structure is freedom. This means that all forms created to dwell in that structure are constituted in freedom. Dwight Hopkins notes:

> Black people longed to be free because they possessed not an ingrained lowliness or willingness toward a white mindset but an inherent and natural gravitation toward freedom. An irrepressible longing to be free engulfed the black community.[18]

Thus freedom is not just a white thing; it is a human thing! The Black struggle for freedom, as Malcolm came to see toward the end of his career, is not ultimately about the right to be Black but the

---

18. Dwight Hopkins, "Slave Theology in the Invisible Institution," in Dwight Hopkins and George C. L. Cummings, eds., *Cut Loose Your Stammering Tongue: Black Theology in the Slave Narratives* (Maryknoll, NY: Orbis Books, 1991), 31.

right to be a child of God, no matter the color of the skin. This is why Malcolm proclaimed, "I believe in human beings, and that all human beings should be respected as such, regardless of their color." Yet because the basis of that oppression has occurred in the context of Black dehumanization, the struggle for human freedom takes on a Black dimension for ultimate relevance.

Given the incompatibility between God's freedom in nature and Black oppression in history, God moves in Black people to mesh history with nature. Given the freedom of the universe's essential structure and God's desire to see a free humanity commensurate with the universe, the yearning for freedom within Black people is a fundamental dimension of their human makeup. Religion, the vehicle by which God is encountered in community, is the path of freedom in the world. Whether the religion be Islam, African traditional religions, or Christianity, freedom is present, despite differing scriptural books, worship, and beliefs. In other words, the foundation of those various expressions of God find their common source in the African quest for freedom. This is why Malcolm made his principal understanding of religion known when he said to his biographer, George Breitman, "I believe in a religion that believes in freedom. Any time I have to accept a religion that won't let me fight a battle for my people, I say to hell with that religion."[19] Religion may be the vehicle but freedom is the goal. This is why, toward the end of his career, he came to see that although formal religious expressions are important, what is more important is articulating the common goal of Black people. He then publicly sought a solution of "common ground" working with anyone of any religion who was sincerely interested in justice for Black people. It was not that he had put down the ideology of separation entirely, and it was certainly not that he no longer saw the bigotry of whites—it was still the biggest obstacle to the achievement of Black humanity! To that point, he did come to see that a battle was inescapable as whites would not render justice voluntarily; the battle had to be waged in

---

19. Malcolm X, *By Any Means Necessary* (New York: Pathfinder, 1992), 172.

bitter and protracted struggle. That struggle would not be waged except through religious faith rooted in freedom and not in hollow ritualistic gestures—a religion that is as public as it is institutional and not just what God was going to do but what humans are compelled to do in a context of acute oppression.

More importantly, Malcolm came to see that trust in God was the most intelligent way to achieve freedom. His newfound theological maturity transcended undying allegiance to a particular methodology, not as a means of escaping the historical suffering of Black people and certainly not as a means of abandoning the Black freedom struggle. He was a realist, through and through, not an escapist. There was, for Malcolm, an inextricable link between religion and freedom, and the authenticity of any religion had to be measured by its commitment to freedom. He was concerned less about pageantry, pomp, pulpit showmanship, and individual wealth, and more concerned about the world Black people were going back into after the benediction. In that sense, Malcolm had demonstrated the theological transcendence necessary to show his love for both his people and for God. He came to see religion as an obstacle to justice if it does not intersect humanity and God in the quest for freedom as its principal goal. But more to our point, Malcolm demonstrated that even though methodologies for freedom and religion are human constructs, their existence cannot be understood apart from the source of the human longing for freedom that informs both—the God of Black liberation! In this sense, the methodology—integration or separation—is not as important as the common end each is seeking—freedom! And for freedom to be realized, trust in God is paramount. But not just any God. It is the God who has created and set Blacks on the path of freedom—to the recognition of Black people as free human beings.

The Accommodationism Challenge

Freedom is not to be compromised. Even in the face of acute hardships inflicted by the white power structure for challenging the legitimacy of white rule, if God's words "Lo, I will be with you until the end of the world" have any meaning, then the pursuit of freedom should not be compromised in any way. As such, Booker T. Washington's program of racial accommodationism represents a prime example of how not to pursue freedom.

To his credit, Washington is to be commended for his humble beginnings as a slave and later as a sharecropper. He should be given kudos for his emphasis on a solid work ethic and agricultural development as a means of Black self-determination. And we are forever indebted to him for his founding of Tuskegee Institute (now University) and his impact on shaping Hampton Institute (now University). Washington became the darling of white Southerners when, on September 18, 1895, he made his famous speech at the Cotton States and International Exposition in Atlanta.[20] Although Washington was a man of deep faith, his strategy for Black progress did not mesh with the God of Black liberation. In fact, racial accommodationism, as evinced in its very nomenclature, is just that—a strategy for Black accommodation, not Black liberation. In other words, Washington did not create a new vision for America rooted in Black freedom. Rather, his approach did little to change the racial landscape. He not only continually ceded power to whites but was content with encouraging Blacks to ingratiate themselves with whites for greater access to the nation's resources. Furthermore, Washington did not favor exposing the racist demographic in America for social change. He instead hoped that if Blacks did not anger whites by publicly denouncing racism and if Blacks maintained a traditional "Protestant work ethic," then whites would eventually grow to accept them.

His philosophy was not lost on white America. He had "earned" the respect of President Theodore Roosevelt so much that he was invited to the White House for dinner in 1901. And even in that, Roosevelt endured harsh criticism for inviting a "Negro" to a place that only white dignitaries graced. Termed a racial moderate for

---

20. It was referred to by W. E. B. Du Bois, Monroe Trotter, and other Black militants as the Atlanta Compromise speech.

most of his public career, Washington was just the type of leader for whom white power elites had been looking.

When Washington left no doubt about his position when he proclaimed that, "the agitation of questions of social equality is the extremest [sic] folly," he all but picked up the gauntlet that Black people had laid down to white America from the holds of ships. Whether Washington intended to increase the number of Black survivors in an era when lynchings had become the new method of Black intimidation or he thought he was sincerely manipulating white power elites for true Black advancement, he did not radically transform Black life in America.

In the first instance—the intention to increase the number of Black survivors in an era when lynchings had become the new method of Black intimidation—it needs to be remembered that in any oppressive context, survival has its place. This is particularly relevant given that making an example out of a few Blacks to send the message that this is what happens when you do not "stay in your place" became commonplace in early twentieth-century America. But when that mentality begins to govern the movement, it produces a social paralysis and emboldens power brokers to continue in their ways. In short, it does not present the oppressor community with a mirror to view its actions and to war with its conscience. In this scenario, opportunistic white power elites can easily massage the Black impact on racial caste and prolong that caste more easily and for much longer than encountering a more uncompromising racial strategy. Fear can paralyze the advancement of a people and has been counted on by whites to preserve power. Despite the devastation of the Black community following the *Plessy* decision making "separate but equal" the law of the land, Washington manipulated the aura in the Black community such that accommodationism parlayed into a tangible contribution to Black progress but not a multigenerational approach that would survive that era. Furthermore, even though a staunch critic of its otherworldliness, Washington's accommodationism also gave theological validity to a "deradicalized" Black church that had begun to abandon Black freedom and to embrace otherworldliness.[21] In short, Washington's accommodationism was able to thrive in a Black community that had begun to wonder if they would ever live in an America of racial justice and whether God was really interested in their freedom.

The fear milieu that catapulted Washington's rise as Black America's premier leader has its biblical precedence in the story of David and Goliath. It was the fear of the Israelites that created the confrontation of David with this marauding giant. The Israelites' lack of faith that God would defeat any obstacle to their freedom blurred their vision and took away their fight for self-determination. David understood that his fellow Israelites had subsumed faith to fear; they "shook and trembled" in the presence of Goliath. Someone had to stand up to Goliath, first in principle, and then in faith. In the end, because David's faith in God was so strong, he did not need the modern advances of weaponry but only needed his trusted slingshot and only one of five stones from a brook to vanquish Goliath and remove the source of fear and trembling from the Israelites. The moral of the story is that faith in the God of the Exodus, who had made a covenant with Abraham, had been reaffirmed. More importantly, David did not seek to make accommodations with Goliath for the sake of Israel's survival. He never believed that Goliath could remain a permanent fixture in Jewish history and genuinely lead the Israelites down the path of freedom that God had forged. He was exclusively concerned with the onward march of Israel, not with currying favor with the Philistines. Goliath's presence as a larger-than-life obstacle to Israelite freedom could have instilled the same fear in David as in the other Israelites, and worse, he could have encouraged the Israelites to seek an accommodationist stance with the Philistines. But he did not. He was singularly focused on removing Goliath from Israelite

---

21. On the "deradicalization" of the Black church at the turn of the twentieth century, see Gayraud S. Wilmore, *Black Religion and Black Radicalism: An Interpretation of the Religious History of African Americans* (Maryknoll, NY: Orbis Books, 1998), 163–95.

life, knowing that it was the only way for freedom to be realized.

In the case of Washington, he prostitutes the Black struggle for freedom. The devastating *Plessy* ruling by the Supreme Court would have been a perfect opportunity to seize the national conscience on the injustice of the decision and to rededicate Black people to the God of Black liberation and the eternity of God's reign. It would have been the perfect opportunity to challenge white America regarding the struggle for full racial equality and to regroup because the God we serve will never let us rest easy with a concession to our full humanity by conceding an America of Black suffering. Like Chicken George from Alex Haley's *Roots*, when he states, "Our sense of hopelessness is our strong point," the devastation of post-Reconstruction America could certainly have served for Washington as leverage to commit Black America more deeply to the *kairos,* or eternal now-ness, of the moment.

In the second instance—the manipulation of white power elites for true Black advancement—even if Washington thought that he was being as sly as a fox in trying to manipulate the white power structure with a "catch-more-flies-with-honey-than-vinegar" approach, it still sacrifices the moral turpitude of the struggle. It suggests that Black people have to resort to chicanery, especially in a postslavery context, to be more cunning than white folks in order to be free. But let's be clear: Black people have always come down on the right side of history in this racial encounter. That is, their oppressed status rendered them no stake in society, making them better able to assess America's moral standing. As such, the protocols of the movement do not have to be watered down or massaged to fit white people's toleration level. In fact, there can be no watered-down assessment of a racist nation! Racism is an immoral institution and could not then nor now be legitimated, despite the best efforts of white Christian leaders to do just that! Black people have been, and continue to be, the conscience of the nation, and when a leader like Washington is unable to recognize the *kairos* of the moment, he forfeits an opportunity to bring America face to face with its conscience and forfeits, more importantly, the religious nature of the path of freedom. In this respect, Joseph Washington notes,

> The Christian faith means nothing if it does not mean sacrifice. But as in the sacrifice of Christ, blood becomes an offering which is no more chosen by human will than is the choosing of a time to be born. When the time comes for blood in order to join human groups into a brotherhood (a free community) it will be a sacrifice—not offered by man of its own free will but in the larger freedom of God—at the *Kairos*, the time God chooses.[22]

In his era, Washington was not able to see that God was calling him to wage a war against the forces that would see Black people continue to be *the punished children of Ham*—a war not of rifles and missiles "but against the rulers, against the authorities, against the cosmic powers of this present darkness, against the spiritual forces of evil in the heavenly places" (Eph 6:12); and in the ultimate biblical dualism, a war not *against* flesh and blood but *for* flesh and blood, for body and soul, for matter and spirit. Joseph Washington notes,

> The single most important human issue is not peace or the absence of war—the destruction of this world by man is within his freedom and is not a deterrent to the Kingdom of God which is in the freedom of God. The presence or absence of war and peace is no guarantee of human degrouping. The fundamental issue is the deghettoizing of the entire Negro group. For the singular restriction of the Negro to the ghetto is the visible reminder of the less obvious ghettos in which all are victimized.[23]

Booker T. Washington is to be commended for imploring us to "cast down your buckets where you are," but the great omission of sacrificing full participation in American life is to take Black people off the path of freedom. It is to forfeit to another generation the task of putting Black people back on the path of

---

22. Joseph R. Washington Jr., *The Politics of God* (Boston: Beacon Press, 1967), 162.

23. Washington Jr., *The Politics of God*, 185.

freedom and surrender for their generation any substantive movement to bridging the chasm between God's freedom in nature and Black freedom in history. He was not able to capture in early twentieth-century America the *Zeitgeist*—the spirit of the times—that Martin Luther King Jr. leveraged in the civil rights movement. Washington could not capture it because the yearning for freedom posited by God was compromised in accommodationism, and the essentially human dimension of the struggle was out of sync with the God of freedom.

Thus, while Washington engaged with racist forces, by accommodating those forces he was undermining the essentially human nature of the Black freedom movement. In short, Washington was content with serving whites more than God—with serving mammon more than freedom. Racism can never be cajoled. It must be faced publicly and with courage in the assured face of white opposition. What Washington missed was that the agitation for social justice espoused by contemporary W. E. B. Du Bois and, before him, Frederick Douglass, Harriet Tubman, Ida B. Wells-Barnett, and Henry McNeal Turner made the type of moral impact on racism that heightened the conscience of America. These Black men and women did more than cast down their buckets; they threw down their gauntlets! They spoke the truth of racism's sinful activity to the powers that benefitted most from it and organized to bring the yang of militant presence to the yin of white privilege. The implications could not be clearer or more crucial. In the context of any immoral governance, the God of freedom calls us not to accommodate it but to destroy it. The goal is to return the human family to its God-given freedom and to a governance rooted in that freedom. That can only happen when Black people leverage the freedom that God has given them and not accommodate racial bigotry but continually attack its right to exist.

God's Freedom and the New Covenant

So often in American history, Black people have been told by white Christian leadership that the achievement of freedom is God's and God's alone and that if God wished Black people to be free from white control, God alone would effectuate that change. The message was clear: insurrections and demonstrations from rabble-rousers seeking to "cause trouble" had no place in Christian faith. To that end, Black people have been taught to see Christian faith concerned primarily with doctrinal rigidity, frequent rituals, and otherworldliness rather than with their freedom. The intent was also clear: to sever Black freedom from Christian faith. In sum, Black people have been told to subsume their freedom to a Christian practice committed to its oppression.

The apostle Paul saw a similar problem when he penned his letter to the church at Galatia. He had grown weary trying to put forward the message of freedom that Jesus brought with the new covenant to an unresponsive church. Paul encountered a church that had forgotten Jesus's message that you need not be enslaved to ritual or confession of sins in order to stave off the wrath of God. The Galatian congregation had fallen prey to the religious tendencies of first-century Palestine, which advocated a faith of frequent temple worship and the presentation of offerings as the cornerstone of Christian practice. But above all, the Galatian church was still observing circumcision as the height of faith expression. As such, the practice of the Galatian church came to mirror the popular faith that Jesus came to nullify in lieu of what should now be the primary goal of the church—freedom!

Paul leaves no doubt as he begins the fifth chapter with the words, "For freedom Christ has set us free. Stand firm, therefore, and do not submit again to a yoke of slavery" (Gal 5:1). Laden in Paul's statement is the primacy of freedom. While he acknowledged that circumcision has its place in Jewish life, it now paled in significance to the freedom imperative of the new Christian faith. Paul is impressing upon the Galatians that the movement to freedom has been inaugurated by God—and that Jesus has freed them to vigorously pursue it. They no longer need to be saddled with the inner struggle of wondering whether you are living a faith that pleases God. One no longer needs to be enslaved to law for when you do so, "you are alienated from Christ; you have fallen away from grace" (5:4). The very grace the Christian is seeking can no longer be found in law; it is found in the concrete freedom given by God to the oppressed.

In every freedom movement for racial justice, there has always been either a sincere objection or an outright defiance from the white community, especially the white Christian community. From plantation insurrections to the civil rights, Black power, and Black Lives Matter movements, Black people have been told that they are either out of sync with God or that they were subverting the natural order of white superiority. Yet, in either case, no matter how sincere, to fight Black people in their struggle for freedom is to fight against the will of God for a free humanity. It is to fall prey to the same theology of the chief priests who resisted rather than embraced the freedom imperative of the new covenant. It is to possess a hardened heart reminiscent of Pharaoh and not possess the liberating Spirit of Jesus. In a virulent twist of fate, the path of freedom is dead-ended by Christian racism rather than illuminated by God's liberating presence. But it is that liberating presence that enables Black people to overcome racist theology and see the path of freedom through to its goal of Black liberation.

> Thus in the very definition of black humanity the yearning for liberation burned like a prairie fire, swift and wide. And nothing, neither white supremacy nor theological heresy, could put out this flame sparking slaves to achieve their God-intended full creativity.[24]

The white church in America has never set well with Black people who proclaimed their freedom to pursue freedom. Like the Galatians, one of the major obstacles to embracing freedom has been institutional religion that trivializes it and emphasizes heavenly reward.

---

24. Hopkins, "Slave Theology in the Invisible Institution," 31.

America has not only been oppressive from its inception but, because of the assumption of Black inferiority, the adoption of a liberating spirit as the cornerstone of Christian life seems as blasphemous as a nonsegregated church! But what white America fails to realize is that the pursuit of freedom on the part of Black people is not Black people's doing. Granted, Black people are the visible human dimension of the struggle, but the process of returning the world to freedom is engineered by the same God whom whites think created white privilege. Furthermore, the historic tension brought about by the prophetic denunciation of racism is not the product of Black people themselves. It is the product of the God of Black liberation who has declared that their time has come.[25] *Chronos* time (historical) and *kairos* time (eternal now) have met at the cross and have been validated in the eternity of God's reign of freedom.

Thus, no matter the obstacles put in Black people's way and the level of trauma inflicted to deter the road to freedom, Black people have been buoyed by God's promise to struggle with them, as exemplified in the name *Immanuel* ("God with us"). This is why whenever Black people were shackled in the holds of ships, they plotted mutiny or committed suicide, for death was preferable to slavery. When whites would not let Black people organize on the plantations, Blacks made their way to the brush arbors in the middle of the night to recommit to freedom. When the Black church "deradicalized," lost its prophetic spirit and became more interested in heaven than earth, Black people created civil rights and nationalist organizations to combat white bigotry and steady themselves for the twentieth-century struggle for liberation. When white media outlets no longer considered racism important and we continued to witness an alarming increase of Black men and women murdered by the police with impunity, Black people bombarded social media with videos of those state-sponsored executions that often do not make the evening news. When white political leadership seeks to convince Americans that we now live

---

25. Hopkins, "Slave Theology in the Invisible Institution," 30.

in a postracial society, despite water contamination in Flint, Michigan, limited access to good health care and education, and income disparities and the re-emergence of white terror groups like the Skinheads and neo-Nazis, Black organizations have boldly claimed to the nation and the world that Black humanity is still a topic of prophetic import.

In the end, it is the oppressed who really matter. For they are the ones who have not been part of the development of power in America but the victims of that power—those of powerless conscience.[26] For only those of powerless conscience with no stake in the nation have the vision to critique the moral pulse of the nation objectively and to articulate it to the world, because they know they are backed by a God who will "prepare a table for them in the presence of their enemies." Only those of powerless conscience have had a liberating encounter with Jesus Christ and have risked life and limb for their posterity. Indeed, they do so at the command and backing of a God who has freed them for the task of freedom.

Finally, Paul maintained that "in Christ Jesus, neither circumcision nor uncircumcision counts for anything; the only thing that counts is faith working through love" (Gal 5:6). Paul is throwing down the theological gauntlet when he uses the normally ill-advised designation of "only." In so doing, he brings a superlative significance to the pursuit of freedom over circumcision as the singular dimension in the life of faith. To this point, one can reasonably conclude that Paul did not have a sentimental or a strictly personal love in mind. Rather, his is a love rooted in the pursuit of freedom as the highest love. It is Paul's *agape* love—an ultimate love. Paul is not interested in a love that preserves the existing situ-

---

26. On the use of the terms "powerless conscience" and "conscience-less power") see the statement of the National Committee of Black Churchmen by radical Black clergy and Black theologians titled "Black Power," in Gayraud S. Wilmore and James H. Cone, eds., *Black Theology: A Documentary History*, vol. 1 (Maryknoll, NY: Orbis Books, 1979), 23–30.

ation. He is interested in a freeing love that is rooted not in social custom but in a new love—a new covenant—that plunges the Christ event squarely in the struggle for human freedom. Paul is letting Galatians know that this demand for freedom was not just relevant for Jesus's life; it is operative in their Galatian context and every other context where oppression exists.

This struggle for human freedom is also the challenge for American Christianity, which is yet to embrace a faith that expresses itself in unconditional love. It too, like the Galatian church, continues to be guided by ritual rather than freedom. It loves the pageantry and liturgy of the church more than Black people's right to be free! Like the chief priests of the time of Jesus and Paul, contemporary Christian leaders, however sincere, are precisely what is wrong with Christian faith in America. They are too often socialized in a Christian orthodoxy grounded in personal relationships, smug piety, and a salvation beyond this world. It is clear that the freedom of Black people is not a priority; it is also clear that Black people, while not sharing fully in American prosperity, should nevertheless feel grateful for the freedoms that they do have. The tragedy, here, is not just in the fact that this sounds more like the chief priests than Jesus but that such an attitude is grounded in racist faith that is ignorant of this theological conflict with Jesus and Paul. Consequently, in opposing the freedom of Black people, American Christianity has misunderstood the new covenant that God brought in Jesus and unwittingly become its enemy.

Just as Paul sounded the bell of freedom in Galatia, Black people have been sounding the bell of freedom for over four hundred years in America. The God of Black liberation will not allow Black people to completely fall prey to white Christian ideology and has kept Black people on the path of freedom. It is the ultimate in "faith expressing itself in love." It is the ultimate religious expression of love—it is indeed *agape* love. Like Paul, Black leaders have been proclaiming that what is needed is a new way of being religious, one that is rooted in Black liberation and not white privilege. This calls for a faith not rooted in ritual but in the love of every human being the way God created them—a love that requires a break with the old covenant and proclaims that Black people deserve to be a part of the threshold of freedom not out of white benevolence but out of God's gratuitous love for creation. What is needed is a new theology that makes freedom the goal of the human family and the pursuit of that freedom the working of God's grace.

That bell of freedom is sounding from the cross, to the church at Galatia, to the holds of slave ships, to auction blocks, to lynching trees, to racist courts, to jail cells, and to this very moment—the *kairos* moment of the fulfillment of the new covenant of freedom. In other words, it is no longer time for a formalistic religion but a militant religion. It is no longer time for a religion that is a pretext for Black oppression but for a religion that is the foundation of a liberating faith that shatters conventional customs of what is considered essentially Christian—essentially religious. It is time to be in solidarity with those of powerless conscience regardless of their religious faith or none at all as it walks the path of freedom that God has laid for them. In short, the God of Black liberation calls us to a conversion experience that is less interested in labels and more interested in freedom.

2

The Path of Conversion

The path of conversion has become a particularly challenging road to travel the more Christianity has become entrenched in tradition. Furthermore, conversion often avoids critical scrutiny and questioning due to its spiritual nature. The conversion event often occurs in the church as converts give their lives to Christ and are introduced to that church's traditions. Yet with Christian faith (and for that matter, all religious faiths) what a convert is taught as the "true" content of faith is at the same time to teach that convert what faith is not. In this latter sense, conversion has had troublesome consequences for Black self-determination.

The Christian convert is generally taught to accept Jesus Christ as one's *personal* Lord and Savior and to develop that personal relationship throughout one's lifetime. That development entails baptism and the practical tasks of a strong prayer life, frequent attendance at worship, with choirs, the usher board, deacon/deaconess boards, missionary committees, and paying one's tithes. Beyond the institutional walls, the convert is implored to adhere to moral prohibitions, especially regarding sexuality, and to refrain from alcohol, cigarettes/cigars, illicit drugs, profanity, and places of ill-repute frequented in our "previous" lives, which are teeming with sin! In fact, the intent is to impress upon the convert that he/she has been adopted by another family, a family different from her biological family, the family of Christ Jesus—the only family that matters! The convert is to understand the new life in God as Spirit filled, that is, to see earthly life as minimally significant and to have a more "spiritual" outlook on life, which is considered to be a brief respite on the trek to the real life of eternity. The end goal of conversion is to be rewarded *personal* salvation in heaven when the days of toiling here on earth are done.

The concern with this approach to conversion is not just what it teaches but what it does *not* teach. It is confined to personal triumph and life in the church and does not extend to global problems nor impress upon the convert how religion itself has contributed to those problems! It presents the religious life in exclusively personal/spiritual terms. Consequently, it teaches the convert to be leery of any other way of seeing faith that deviates from that understanding of faith. Thus, faith is presented as a call to socio-political change—evident, for example, in the Exodus narrative of a people moving from slavery to freedom at God's behest; it has been looked upon as an anomaly at best and as just irreligious at worst. An approach to faith that includes human oppression is either sinful or viewed as a necessary obstacle but has no place in the life of the church. This becomes particularly disconcerting in a context in which human oppression has existed for hundreds of years and Christian theology has, not surprisingly, contributed to its legitimacy by its very emphasis on the religious individual rather than the body politic. In short, it leads the convert to think that God is not concerned with the state of humanity beyond church walls and that those who seek to make faith inclusive of human freedom should be looked upon with great suspicion. If white Protestant churches failed to be a beacon of leadership in America's racial crisis, part of the responsibility for the failure was due to the way its leading spokespersons ignored race in their interpretation of the Christian faith.[1] It is those leading spokespersons of Christian faith who have been "programmed" to see faith in personal and otherworldly structures and therefore, by inference, "programmed" to condemn any person or group who seeks to reconfigure faith in a more liberating way. But more importantly, it is those leading

---

1. James H. Cone, *The Cross and the Lynching Tree* (Maryknoll, NY: Orbis Books, 2011), 57.

spokespersons of Christian faith, who, by church custom, teach converts to think in a similar theological fashion. One reason for this is that the church has committed itself to be more of a place of personal refuge and wish-fulfillment than a strategic center for liberating change. As a result, mass movements in oppressive contexts have not found a solid footing in the church. Thus, what we have come to know as orthodox Christianity has been little more than an unashamed call to maintain existing social conditions. What has this meant for Christian theology? It has resulted in a church governed by the God of white racism rather than the God of Black liberation.

Conversion and Christian Freedom

Certainly, this traditional approach to conversion stemmed from the theological understanding of white pastors and theologians of slavery as an eternal institution. In other words, Black people were not converted to the Christian faith to be Christians but rather to be meek slaves. That commitment to Black oppression raised two crucial questions for white Christian leadership regarding their understanding of human freedom: Is slaveholding un-Christian and does baptizing slaves parlay into freedom? First, white Christian leaders assured slaveholders that not only is slaveholding not a violation of faith but that taking heathen West Africans into slavery should be regarded as the height of Christian stewardship. Given their heathen ontology, their enslavement should be seen as a salvific opportunity to expose Africans to civilization and find favor with God. Given this theological validation, white slaveholders were emboldened to continue in the slavocracy. Second, to prevent baptism from getting linked with freedom, the task was to construct a "legitimate" theology such that it extolled human freedom but not Black people's freedom from the slavocracy. This became particularly crucial after the Christianizing process of slaves began in the late eighteenth century. Bishop Berkeley's famous letter to the colonists in 1727 concerning freedom stated that the Christian faith frees one from inner demons such as lust and sex, but "does not make the least alteration in property," and "continues them (slaves) in the same condition as before." Therefore, "as to their outward condition, their becoming Christians and being baptized makes no manner of change in it."[2]

White Christian ministers used this interpretation of Christian freedom ad nauseam in sermons and catechisms, and it has become the very fabric of how Christian faith is understood and lived—a faith that was decidedly paternalistic, personal, spiritual, and otherworldly. As far as white planters were concerned, God had spoken and had given full approval for the slavocracy and, more importantly, legitimized the dehumanization of Black people as an expression of Christian life. A new era of Christian faith emerged that was doggedly protective of its personal, highly interior, and highly otherworldly structure. With conversion being the primary foundation, the intent was to affirm white Christian bigotry throughout eternity and rob Black people of any foundation for a theology that would change their earthly condition, such as a theology of Black liberation.

After several generations and hundreds of years, conversion came to mean a commitment to faith as an "inward condition." To this end, while conversion has been looked upon as one of the more pivotal moments in one's faith journey, it has been acutely oppressive in its very structure and, as a result, debilitating to a liberation imperative in both white and Black churches. Conversion has been debilitating in the white church insofar as it legitimates white superiority. By not making the world of oppressive relationships a key component of faith, it does not call whites to conscience about the highly oppressive way in which they have used Black people as commodities to obtain wealth and status. In this sense, wealth and morality have been virulently intertwined.

---

2. See Bishop of London George Berkley's highly influential letter from 1727 on baptism and Christian freedom addressed "to the Masters and Mistresses of Families in the English Plantations Abroad; Exhorting Them to Encourage and Promote the Instruction of Their Negroes in the Christian Faith."

Conversion calls whites to very little reckoning prophetically regarding the *imago dei* in Black people. This in turn leads to internalizing stereotypes of Black humanity as criminally innate and lacking industry which, in turn, justifies insulation of whites from Blacks. But more importantly, it gives white Christians the divine approval to continue to develop sermons, publish devotional materials, sing hymns, and issue prayers in the personal, spiritual, and otherworldly terms that have come to characterize Christian faith in the Western hemisphere. Speaking in his Latin American context, theologian Juan Luis Segundo expresses a similar concern.

> Mass is the only bond relating the average Christian to God. This mass is characterized by unvarying liturgical elements, pre-established readings, an unchanging Eucharistic service, and the eternal return to the same feasts on the yearly liturgical calendar. In short, it represents the polar opposite of a religion based on historical sensitivity.[3]

This view, in large part, informs the white mentality that frowns on Black freedom movements in history and other deviations from tradition as demonic, anti-American, and ungodly. In short, conversion is ideological for the white church in that it leaves "theological wiggle room" for whites to be both Christian and racist.

Conversion is ideological in the Black church in that it leaves "theological wiggle room" to be oppressed and Christian at the same time! It also covets a conversion experience that honors personalism, spirituality, and otherworldliness held by the white church and revels in its theological conservatism, dogmatic rigidity, and anti-liberation worldview. While we can certainly conclude that the Black church is far more demonstrative emotionally than the white church, as the shouts and the pastoral whoop have been staple parts of the Black church experience, its theological language is remarkably similar to the white church. In this sense, conversion is too! Thus, while white pastors have been remarkably

---

3. Juan Luis Segundo, *The Liberation of Theology* (Maryknoll, NY: Orbis Books, 1976), 40.

silent on racism, sexism, and poverty, Black pastors have, for the most part, been similarly situated, and some have arrogantly maintained that the pulpit is not the place for "social and Black stuff." Joseph Washington notes,

> This realm is deemed the practical politics of men and is not questioned as to whether it patterns itself after the practical politics of God. Negro folk religion has become the partial captive of the immediate success-worship of white devils in blackface.[4]

The language of the sermons, songs, prayers, and the message/images of devotional materials of most Black churches mirror those of the white church. Jesus is still white, and teaching materials still tend to be imaged by white and not Black characters. Because Black Christians have unconsciously internalized the language of the white church, the Black church has given little direct attention to the racism its congregations suffer in the nation and world, and to the sexism women experience in the society *and* church with many of those Black Protestant ministers operating out of the Catholic custom that denies the ministry to women.

> What does this mean? To the majority of Christians, it undoubtedly means that God is more interested in nontemporal things than in solutions for the historical problems that are cropping up. And it is too much to ask the average Christian, who is subject to such strong theoretical and practical pressure, to detach his scale of values from what seems to be the religious realm *par excellence* in order to associate it with another type of activity in the name of Christianity itself.[5]

In this religious milieu, what seldom comes to the forefront of discussion is the unwillingness or inability to deviate from conventionality and embrace a faith inclusive of historical movements for

---

4. Joseph R. Washington, *The Politics of God* (Boston: Beacon Press, 1967), 168.
5. Segundo, *The Liberation of Theology*, 40–41.

freedom. The convert is introduced to a faith that is more comforting and less militant, to a church that is still tending toward refuge and not change, toward endurance and not conscience!

The danger in this understanding of faith for Black people is that white Christian indoctrination is still very much a part of the life of the Black church. While the Black church has been instrumental in instilling in Blacks that God created us equal to all other people, despite white pronouncements to the contrary, with each service, Bible study, prayer meeting in which Blacks do not familiarize themselves with their history, American history, African history, and racial and gender history, they are forfeiting an opportunity to create a more responsible and historically enlightened faith community. When there is no mention of Christian faith's connection to the Exodus narrative and to Jesus as a liberator of people who were in the very condition Black people face, we are forfeiting an opportunity to forge a liberating conversion experience. Whenever we gather and stay arrogantly in our homophobic and personal worldview, we are not preparing our congregations for a life with the God of Black liberation! In our sincere intent, we are normalizing for our converts an asocial, ahistorical religious approach that serves the interests of the white power structure more than the freedom of Black people. But more importantly, Black people continue to exist in a paternalistic relationship with the white community that does not compel Blacks to deal decisively with the theological dimension of white superiority. This leads to an unwitting contentment with a negative self-image that makes God a panacea that hastens Black people's dash to the church to "turn it over to the Lord."

But the God of Jesus Christ, the God of Black liberation, is a co-struggling partner who frowns on escapist worship. God will not liberate a people who will not seek to liberate themselves. Frowning on history and arrogantly thinking that God will change one's condition emerges from a context in which a people's self-image has been severely mutilated.

> The Negro people have failed to take seriously the experience of Israel and the relentless call to God, who is faithful

to His purpose. Negro people wish to interpret freedom and equality in the context of white culture and wish it to be demonstrated through their own rise in middle class representation. Thereby Negroes shun their call to free the white preconscious here and everywhere in order that all men may be free for the Kingdom.[6]

That white preconscious is not shunned since most Black congregations do not realize that they are still expressing faith under the canopy of white approval. Ascension into the white middle class is still seen as the cornerstone of American success, with very little thought given to the concept of tokenism and even less to the continued discriminatory practice of Black underrepresentation in the place of employment. In this sense, the highly individualistic aspect of Christian indoctrination is clearly manifest to the detriment of the larger Black community and to the service of white privilege.

They desire a stake in this country for the understandably human purposes of personal satisfaction rather than for ultimate social change which may bring more than a mere realignment of human power. The fascination with immediate successes leads to the comforting delusion of individual achievements based on the assumptions of white rationalizations, which are themselves in need of redemption.[7]

This is precisely why the Black church needs a new approach to conversion that entails a more indigenous learning curve rooted in liberation for the voiceless and marginalized than either the white church or the Black church can deliver in their current configurations.

Conversion Seeking Truth

Invariably, the questions will arise: Should not the theology of the Black church and the white church look the same? Given their

---

6. Washington, *The Politics of God*, 168–69.
7. Washington, *The Politics of God*, 169.

shared universal faith, Christianity, should not the theological emphases, language, and worship be similar? And given that white and Black people have lived in the same country now for over four hundred years, should not their approach to faith be the same? My answer is a resounding no! The white church arose out of a sense of white privilege and contempt for blackness, so it stands to reason that such a grotesque view of darker human beings would find its way into its theology. But the Black church, in response to that imposition of oppression, should not mirror the white church but be the opposite—especially theologically. Even though the races have lived in the same nation and, furthermore, in close proximity to each other, Black people have had to deal with the unnecessary trauma inflicted by white people and existentially wonder what—other than the color of their skin—they have done to deserve it. Physical proximity does not take into account the totally disparate historical experiences of each race brought on primarily by the actions of white people. In fact, such proximity was necessary to create the disparate historical experiences. Thus, conversion to the same faith should not look the same in its lived applications. The God of white supremacy is pleased with white people's interactions with Black people, but the God of Black liberation is highly displeased. The God of Black liberation calls for the destruction of the current theological house that glorifies Black dehumanization beginning with the conversion and, thereafter, the way faith is taught and practiced.

The first task of a revamped conversion experience must be uncovering the truth of African/Black history. Jesus proclaimed, "You will know the truth, and the truth will make you free" (John 8:32) and advocated that a faith in which freedom is intrinsic to its core should not openly promote the enslavement of any race of people. Given that white privilege has been built on untruths about Black humanity and African culture, any relevant theology must seek to deconstruct those untruths so that we can live in a nation structured on truth and not the falsehoods that have created superior and inferior mentalities. Conversion must be about a faith that exposes those falsehoods of white Christian leadership and intellectuals about Black people and infuse into Black people a self-image not rooted in white racial mythology. The conversion process must be restructured so that it impresses upon the convert that the new life of faith is a commitment to reimaging the liberating essence of being a Christian. It is an earthly call to be a voice for the least of these in our generation as it was for Jesus in his generation. In the Christian tradition, what often gets lost in the conversion experience is that Jesus was not looking for the convert to praise him necessarily but to emulate him in his absence. Thus, the life of Jesus was not meant to be a historical moment but a paradigm for change; a paradigm for change that is committed to bringing truth into a world of mistruths—a truth that frees! This is the meaning of the new covenant.

Given the current Christian faith that has linked whiteness with divinity, not surprisingly, the task at hand is to put it on a permanent trash heap and proceed with the question, what does it mean to be Black and Christian? Or more to the point, how is Black humanity to be reimaged out of the centuries of false depictions by white scholars? Those questions should not be seen as unrelated; but if, in fact, the truth of the God of Black liberation will set us free then no Christian theology can be relevant in our time without departing from those questions. They have been given ultimate import not only in making Black people slaves but doing so no less in the name of God. Thus, the key to understanding the true meaning of faith lies in bringing a corrective to a racist Christianity by uncovering those falsehoods that prevent a free Black humanity from emerging.

To this end, Black humanity needs to be positively reimaged, beginning with a more liberating and favorable view of African culture. The fact that the devaluing of Africa made it into Christian theology is not surprising. It has made the more truthful presentation of Africa more formidable as it challenges the European accusation of heathenism and thus the reasonability to enslave on Christian grounds. The Christianization of African slaves itself came at a much later date in the slavocracy when planters were somewhat convinced by white ministers that it was not detrimental to the slavocracy for slaves to be both slaves and Christian. Thus, it was not for the sake of righteousness that slaves were Christianized but to make them better tools for economic exploitation. Thus, the Christian missionary movement took on a positive role in converting Africans to faith, but the intent was never to produce a free African but a Christian African.[8] With only inward freedom built in to the theology of the white church, becoming a Christian African meant a relinquishing of the freedom that biblical revelation affirmed. Learning how to be a Christian from white Christians meant learning a faith that subverted the very end goal of God—freedom! Thus, conversion to faith under the canopy of whiteness was not a call to freedom but a call to eternal marginalization.

As the remembrance of African history died with the first generations of slaves, the seasoning process began to take root. With little positive remembrance of African culture, Black people became ashamed of their blackness, with many internalizing white depictions of African culture as subhuman and uncivilized and struggling to feel a greater sense of their humanity as they tried to ascend into the good graces of white people. Far too many Black people tend to have an extremely negative view of Africa and its cultural expressions and have settled on a European worldview that stifles Black freedom and self-determination. It suffices for some Black people, and Black Christians in particular, that Africa is cultural "dead weight," and the key to "successful" living is to forsake the greater rise of the community and seek a life that only caters to their immediate family's well-being. What Black people fail to

---

8. See Forrest G. Wood, *The Arrogance of Faith: Christianity & Race in America from the Colonial Era to the Twentieth Century* (Boston: Northeastern University Press, 1990); Joseph R. Washington Jr., *Anti-Blackness in English Religion: 1500–1800* (New York: Edwin Mellen Press, 1984); C. Eric Lincoln, *Race, Religion and the Continuing American Dilemma* (New York: Hill & Wang, 1984); Eugene D. Genovese, *A Consuming Fire: The Fall of the Confederacy in the Mind of the White Christian South* (Athens, GA: University of Georgia Press, 1998); and Albert Raboteau, *Slave Religion: The "Invisible Institution" in the Antebellum South* (New York: Oxford University Press, 1978).

realize about this mentality is that their image of Africa comes from the same white explorers and scholars who advocated Black subordination. The intent, no doubt, is to make what is good, valued, and proper emerge only out of European culture; to establish white male thinking as normative and white culture as superior. White Christian leadership did not condemn this obvious violation of faith. Rather, it touted the inextricable link between white superiority and divine wisdom.

It becomes apparent why any new approach to conversion had to have a diminished historical component. While white historians and other scholars did their part in presenting Black people as a wayward animalistic people whom white folks should be commended for enslaving, there was the possibility that Black people would discover the truth about their ancestors. In the event that some "militant" Black people would emerge seeking a more truthful view of Africa, the hope was that the teaching of Africa's barbarity over several generations would have had enough of an impact on Black people's self-image to keep them from seeing any virtue in African culture.

The white community's concern that Black people would adopt a more favorable image of themselves was that it would severely limit white people's ability to keep them in contented captivity. The clarion call to freedom made by African American leaders, many of whom were ministers and saw their calling as bringing liberation to their people, might be internalized by the masses, and a Christian faith that addresses Black oppression could become the new Christian norm. In this sense, linking the struggle of Black people with its religious faith is crucial for its relationship with God and with one another. Such faith affirms the history of struggle from slavery to postslavery and postsegregation, and God's majestic presence in those victorious movements. It also affirms that the Black struggle is the contemporary example of Israel's exodus to freedom. What has this meant for conversion? When void of the connection between Israel's freedom in the Bible and Black people's struggle for freedom today, the conversion experience is inauthentic in that it seeks a "reborn" Christian without a positive history of Africa.

To its credit, the Black church seeks to instill a sense of "somebodyness" through positive reinforcement in conversion. But it seeks to do so without deeply immersing the convert in the true history of his/her culture. Consequently, the Black church falls prey to the universalism of the white church by naïvely thinking that one can be a true child of God while possessed of a deformed racial self-image. In so doing, the static conservatism of the Black church is at odds with freedom movements and prophetic leaders who are able to judge rightly that the freedom of Blacks cannot come through a rejection of one's history, whether intentional or not. So when a Black convert proudly proclaims, "I have had an encounter with Jesus," the retort has to be, "Which Jesus?" Is it the Jesus of white supremacy or the Jesus of Black liberation? The former has promoted Black second-class citizenship, but the latter has proclaimed freedom for Blacks. The former has not been the cure for Black people who have come from the holds of slave ships to their current standing. The latter has come in the truth of the history of African life and is the human embodiment of Black liberation. Such a truth has not come through spirited worship services and spine tingling singing and preaching but through an affirmation of Black people being free Christians and proud Africans. It has also come through a liberating conscience given by God to never tire of deconstructing white theories about Black bodies.

This is why the learning of African/Black history is crucial for a healthy Black self-image—one that does not emerge from white theologians. Their world is guided by the God of white supremacy and given over to Black inferiority. It stands to reason, then, that their perspectives will directly or indirectly tout the virtues of continued Black subjugation. It is illogical to think that an ahistorical approach to faith can be overcome by another ahistorical approach to faith that teaches Black people that freedom will come if they simply continue in their ritualistic, otherworldly ways. Black people are able to opt out of being a Christian but not being Black. Black history precedes Black people wherever they go and has been presented negatively in a world ruled by white privilege. But given the liberating message of biblical revelation, those Black people who have maintained their Christian affiliation must make their way through these two poles (Black and Christian), and both must be affirming in their liberating essence, not intertwined in racist pedagogy. In other words, both must be given positive virtue in their initial presentation. *There must be a liberating worldview in Christian faith,* and *there must also be a humanizing treatment of African/Black culture.* It is the Black way of saying that white scholars and theologians do not have the last say in how Black people view faith and how they view their blackness. To be Black and Christian demands both. That means a holistic history of African affirmation and a Christian theology that holds for the least of these, the voiceless, and the despised, a liberating destiny consistent with biblical revelation. For this to happen, the conversion process must reorient the thinking that Christian life lies in how well one performs liturgical customs or how well one sings or preaches. Furthermore, the convert must understand that the "apprenticeship" of faith demands a commitment to transforming Christian practice to reflect its liberating essence and to declare to Black people that, where their condition is concerned, the God of Black liberation is not neutral.

Conversion, Preaching, and Militant Religion

The church's continued emphasis on the religious individual, the spirit, and otherworldliness stifles a liberation hermeneutic from blossoming. It prevents the establishment of a militant religion. This is not pure happenstance. This is because the convert is generally taught that Christian faith has no socio-political dimension and therefore does not extend to human liberation. It mostly limits the religious individual to his/her financial and health statuses in this world and the ecstasy that awaits in the next world.

Long acknowledged as the backbone of the life of the church, preaching reinforces the tenets of Christian teaching about conversion. Through preaching, the convert is exposed to the meaning of Christian experience and how God is encountered. Throughout the history of the Black church, preaching has been the tonic that compelled Black people to "keep on keepin' on," despite tremendous obstacles and perpetual setbacks. Yet, that same sermonic language has been more ideological than transformative in the sense that it has not sought to heighten consciousness of Black oppression. It has avoided the language of liberation. It has not been persistent in articulating the encounter with God as the encounter with systemic evil. Before anything else, sermonic language has been more emotionally arousing than affirming of freedom. To be sure, this approach to sermonic language by Black preachers has had an element of survival for its parishioners in the face of white backlash, but theologically, there has also been an unwitting capitulation to the language of the white church.

This highly dramatic and entertaining approach of Black preaching began on the plantation, where white ministers insisted on an expression of faith that would make slaves contented and desired a Christian language that would keep Black slaves happily oppressed. They concluded that this goal could be accomplished if the messages were delivered with unbridled conviction and delivered by someone Black. In this way, slaves would let down their guard and be more receptive to the message. Thus began an approach to preaching that would teach unlearned Black ministers the rudiments of white-controlled sermonic language and provide them with a theology of Black subordination rather than one of liberation. It was only on this condition that the white Christian establishment felt more comfortable that Black preachers would not preach sermons with direct references to freedom from slavery.[9]

People in the slave community acquiesced, since it allowed them Sundays off to worship God, even if it were ultimately the God of white supremacy. Their hope was that they could get that day off, enjoy getting dressed up and being with other Black people in a nonwork environment, and experience God without conforming

---

9. See Charles Colcock Jones, *The Religious Instruction of Negroes in the United States* (Savannah, GA: Thomas Purse Publishing, 1842); also Eugene D. Genovese, *Roll Jordan Roll: The World the Slaves Made* (New York: Vintage Books, 1976).

to the dictates of white Christianity. Unfortunately, this did not happen. For even though there were slaves who did not buy into the theology of white supremacy, the Christian message took on a more personal and otherworldly tone and eventually became the unquestioned language in both the white and Black churches.[10]

Seldom are the words racism, sexism, poverty, homophobia, and Islamophobia mentioned in church language. Biblical themes of liberation in the Exodus narrative, the Hebrew boys in the fiery furnace, Daniel in the lions' den, Paul's affirmation of human freedom, and Jesus's proclamation of God's reign as one of socio-political liberation have become a rarity in sermonic/church language. In most instances, a sermon that is deeply rooted in racial history or is a prophetic critique of contemporary racism is regarded as a homily but not true preaching. The general response from most parishioners when hearing a sermon that prophetically condemns racial division is: "It was great, and we need to hear more of it," but such preaching is ultimately branded in most church circles as "social stuff." More pointedly, a sermon deeply prophetic and progressive is deemed incendiary and not in keeping with traditional preaching. In fact, "good" preaching has meant staying firmly inside the paradigm of white theological acceptance—rooted in personal wish-fulfillment to accentuate the spiritual dimension of faith and to rejoice at the "saints'" triumphal entry into the kingdom—and divorced from social change. Emotions of congregants are better aroused in this fire-and-brimstone style of preaching, and the more freedom-affirming, historically grounded sermon is usually commended but not preferred. Indeed, it is a foreign concept! The kingdom is seldom related to the end of white privilege and the beginning of human equality in this world.

This distortion of language affected even Martin Luther King Jr. Though progressive in his own way, young King admitted later in life that he struggled with Daddy King's preaching, which tended

---

10. James H. Cone, *Black Theology & Black Power* (Maryknoll, NY: Orbis Books, 1989), 91–115.

toward fire and brimstone and not toward the condition of Black people. So intense was this struggle that young King was beginning to debate whether his ministerial calling was authentic insofar as he had not seen from Black church leaders, including his father, the kind of preaching that sought to evince a change in the way Black people thought about God and how whites treated Blacks. Young King found this style of preaching disappointing, considering that the period represented the height of racial segregation and symbols of that bigotry were overt. Even as a pre-teenager, the prophetic conscience, the drum major instinct, corralled King's spirit, but he did not get the reinforcement he was seeking in the liturgical life of Ebenezer Baptist Church in Atlanta where his father pastored. This led King to "table" his commitment to ministry, wondering whether it would ever be resumed. In retrospect, it is not too much to say that we almost lost one of our greatest articulators of the Black condition due to the language of the church not mirroring in context or biblical revelation the liberation imperative inherent in Christian theology.[11] It was not until King matriculated at Morehouse College at age fifteen[12] and shared his struggle with then-president Benjamin Elijah Mays, who assured young King that his call was indeed authentic and that we needed more aspiring ministers of his theological persuasion, that King picked up his ministerial gauntlet once again, and this time until death. It was on President Mays's admonition that King went on to a doctorate degree in systematic theology and to a distinguished public career as a minister who forever changed the racial landscape of America. King would discover a continuation of that language deficiency in Montgomery during the bus boycott in 1955 and his dismissal

---

11. Stephen B. Oates, *Let the Trumpet Sound: The Life of Martin Luther King, Jr.* (New York: Plume Publishing, 1982).

12. Besides being promoted to a higher grade because of his high academic achievement, King was allowed to enter Morehouse at fifteen because Black colleges were experiencing low enrollment due to World War II. The acceptance was pending proficiency on an entrance exam, which King passed. See Oates, *Let the Trumpet Sound*, 6.

The Path of Conversion | 49

from the National Baptist Convention by the more conservative pastor and then-president J. H. Jackson.[13]

King serves as a prime example as to how Christian language has remembered him in history. King is referred to more by historians and ministers as a civil rights activist than a minister or religious leader. The reason is obvious: for far too many white and Black Christians, Christian language has retained its "spiritual" and otherworldly status and has become even more deeply entrenched in a so-called postracial society where there is supposedly no more systemic racism. The extent of racism is characterized as only episodic at best and is more a figment of Black people's imagination than an accurate reflection of contemporary America. Thus, white America is still aggressively seeking to divorce itself from its continued participation in white privilege, and the church is still imprisoned in a language that prevents that bigotry from the prophetic condemnation that the God of Black liberation demands.

The reality is that church language has not prophetically denounced socio-political oppression as a norm and, not surprisingly, has had a huge impact on both the aspiring minister enamored by the pulpit showmanship of preachers, and the recent convert who is convinced that the life of the church as currently constituted represents Christian practice in its totality. The reckoning of conscience that should be a staple part of Christian language fails to get a proper hearing, and hundreds of thousands, even millions, of converts come into the fold without confronting the question of Black humanity and its quest for liberation. The goal of faith has been to be a "good Christian," or what Mays

---

13. See, in particular, King's deep concern for the conservative theology of many Black pastors and its impact on their involvement in movements for social change in his book *Stride toward Freedom: The Montgomery Story* (San Francisco: Harper & Row Publishers, 1958), 11–29. King was eventually dismissed from the National Baptist Convention by its then-President J. H. Jackson, who saw King's social involvement as contrary to the core values of the convention. The split over ideology eventually led to the formation of the Progressive National Baptist Convention.

refers to as "a Christian in my heart" but not to be a free human being—a free human being not just subjectively but objectively; in other words, a free human being not in Bishop Berkeley's "inward" worldview but a free human being in Christ, and that is a free human being in society. To this end, we must never lose sight of the fact that a Christian conversion that "does not make the least alteration in civil relations" or baptism that "makes no manner of change" in one's outward condition is *the* grand distortion of the gospel. Being "a Christian in my heart" is not only to proclaim that one is free in Jesus—to do so would only be to remain within the confines of white Christian thinking. The meaning of faith, however, is to realize freedom in history.

Conversion and the Black Christ

The conversion process must not omit the God of Black liberation's incarnation. The Christian convert must be introduced to the Black Jesus. That Black Jesus proclaimed, "I am the way, and the *truth*, and the life" (John 14:6). True conversion, then, is through him, and "his truth must march on." The locale of that march to freedom is history. But Christian truth does not apply simply to a hodgepodge of historical events but to how those events are judged through the lens of the Christ event. In other words, we come to understand the meaning and goal of history as we measure its events through the life of Jesus. This means first learning the truth about the standard of truth—Jesus.

That truth bears us witness that Jesus was indeed a Black man from Africa and not a white man from Europe! Numerous attempts to connect Jesus to Europe have failed miserably. Attempts have even been made by white theologians and biblical scholars to change geography and claim that northeast Africa, where Jesus was born, was during the time of Jesus's birth a part of southeastern Europe and was annexed to Africa after Jesus's death. Yet there is no credible historical and geopolitical proof that can establish such a "fact." Biblical revelation records Jesus and his mother fleeing to Egypt to escape Herod, who had put out a death sentence on Jesus when he received word that Jesus could be the son of humanity. Egypt was never a geographical area of the world inhabited by those of European descent, and the fact that Jesus and his mother were running there to blend in with the Egyptians means that Jesus had to have been a man of color and not a white man.

The fact of the matter is that Jesus was an African Hebrew who became despised by the Pharisees, scribes, and chief priests for bringing a "new" theology of God's primary concern for the disinherited. In this light, they had tremendous difficulty dealing theologically with John the Baptist's claim that the advent of the man who would become the messiah for the world was an African Hebrew and, more importantly, in their midst. The reasoning is that no God would choose to become a human given the virtual insignificance of the affairs of the world let alone come to the most despised people according to the wealthy, tax collectors, and religious leaders. If there were an incarnation, then certainly God would come to someone whose humanity and culture were superior and occupied the top rungs of the social, economic, and political ladder. Yet, because the God of Black liberation takes the logic of the privileged and stands it on its head, God makes the divine decision, in like manner to creating all humans in freedom, to make right with the world what Adam and Eve had made wrong. This is why Jesus is referred to as the second Adam. For through one man has sin entered into the world, so too by one man shall humanity be redeemed (Rom 5:12). Indeed, Jesus took on the atoning role of the world with his death but identified directly with the despised, the lowly, and the oppressed. Essentially, the affairs of humans are important to God; and, if the Lukan proclamation of "release of the captives" is true, then the liberation of the oppressed is the matrix through which the will of God is to be seen. And it is precisely because of the incarnation that allegiance to the oppressed is seen both in Jesus's physical identification and in his theological outlook. This is the beginning of truth that the path of conversion reveals.

Theologian Karl Barth is correct in noting that the key to understanding Christian faith lies not in religion nor in humanity acting as if it were God. In fact, it lies in the revelation of God in Jesus that points us to the intersection between time and eternity. Yet Barth did not go far enough. That revelation entails more than a universal forgiveness of sins but is principally concerned with the least of these—the voiceless and the dispossessed—and with fashioning a new humanity in history that seeks an end to oppressor–oppressed relationships.[14] In other words, the Christ event is concerned not just with the condition of an individual or the bank account of a church but is fundamentally concerned with the societal treatment of human beings ostracized from the fullness of national and global life not just during Jesus's life but throughout human history. The grace of God seen in the incarnation is not concerned with biblical literalism as a point of profound faith, nor an extensive knowledge of the inessentials of the Bible (i.e., how many chapters, verses, etc.), but with its principal meaning of liberation. This meaning extends beyond biblical history to modern history wherein the Christ event's enduring relevance is found. As Cone affirms,

> The authority of the Bible for Christology, therefore does not lie in its objective status as the literal Word of God. Rather it is found in its power to point to the One whom the people have met in the historical struggle for freedom. Through our reading of scripture, the people not only hear stories about Jesus that enable them to move beyond the privacy of their own story; but through faith because of divine grace, they are taken from the present to the past and then thrust back into their contemporary history with divine power to transform the socio-political context.[15]

---

14. See Juan Luis Segundo, *A Theology for Artisans of a New Humanity*, 5 vols. (Maryknoll, NY: Orbis Books, 1973). The very title of the series contains the intentionality of the liberation project's emphasis on a new way of doing theology that is designed to bring about a new humanity, a liberated humanity.

15. James H. Cone, *God of the Oppressed* (New York: Seabury Press, 1975), 112.

Cone demonstrates how the crux of the Christ event has ultimate meaning in our time. Given that American imperialism has operated much like first-century Palestine, with its claims of superpower status and superior thinking, it forms an intrinsic connection to Black people's struggle for freedom. For just as Jesus came with a message from a God, who is first and foremost a liberator, Black people no longer need to look simply at Jesus as savior of their individual sins or to find Jesus's work in the personal and spiritual realms of human experience alone. Rather, just as Jesus challenged a sin-sick world for the salvation of humanity, he also brought that sin-sick world face to face with its conscience. This is the primary reason he was crucified. Yet he came as a liberator for the Jews, or the "lost sheep of Israel," as he advised his disciples, and for this salvific work, he came primarily for those exploited and abused the most. This central aspect of his ministry cannot be rendered a footnote of biblical history lest faith become a pretext for human commodification. But because the political and religious leaders of his time had become so deeply entrenched in its distorted faith and political decisions that benefited a few to the detriment of the many, he was sent to the electric chair of his time for supposedly engaging in a treasonous act. He was viewed not as a liberator but as a threat to privileged existence, a rabble-rouser, an antagonist. That historical lynching happened for one reason: Jesus had assumed complete solidarity with the oppressed; and, because he was God incarnate, it affirmed God's solidarity as well. This is why in contemporary America, God has identified with a people who have been robbed of everything sacred to any people—names, languages, culture, religion, and God—and have suffered at the crack of the whip, the stage of the auction block, the burning smell of flesh on a lynching tree, and languishing in prisons serving excessive sentences for no other reason than their blackness. And because of that historical reality, God becomes Black in our time as he became Jewish in first-century Palestine, making the world know through the incarnation that the creator God and the liberator God are one and the same.

What appears to be reverse racism for some is in reality the new covenant. God brings the new covenant in Jesus to signal an end to the primacy of ritual and to shift it to the primacy of struggle—to champion the primacy of protest against Black oppression and to usher in the day when struggle for Black liberation is seen not as incendiary but salvific. For in the words of Kelly Brown Douglas, "If God identifies with Black people and sustains them in their struggle for freedom, and if Jesus offers a freedom that is attainable in history, then it is appropriate—if not required—for Christians to rebel against any social barrier to Black people's freedom."[16] In response to Douglas's "if not required," I offer, "required!" It is the God-commanded duty to rebel against any structures that prevent Black humanity from blossoming in the way God created.

In our time, no other people fit the bill of a despised people, a people who have had their ancestry, their cultural expressions, their aesthetic features, and their demand to be full participants in society, mocked, ridiculed, and hindered more than Black people. No other race of people has suffered unduly for now over four hundred years of racial imperialism than Black people. Therefore, no other people can lay claim to a Black Jesus and a Black God—a God of Black liberation—more than Black people in America!

In sum, the path of conversion makes the community aware of this racist Christian history and the misrepresentation of Jesus. This misrepresentation would have Black converts see the God of Black liberation as blasphemous, but not a white Jesus; holds for a universal salvation for all, but are comfortable with separate white and Black churches; holds for a God focused on heaven, while they create hell for Black people on earth; and holds for the primacy of sexual morality, but not the primacy of racial morality. To effectively incorporate the being and ministry of Jesus into a vibrant Christian theology is to sacrifice white superiority at the altar of truth, which is Jesus! Thus, the path of conversion must first and foremost acknowledge that the faith has been committed less to human liberation and more to white privilege. In this

---

16. Kelly Brown Douglas, *The Black Christ* (Maryknoll, NY: Orbis Books, 1994), 43.

sense, Christian faith has represented the worst of humanity and therefore misrepresented the creator God. "A theology that sanctions slavery savors too strongly of Satan to be tolerated. . . . The religion of Jesus Christ has nothing in common with the auction block or the lash."[17] Furthermore, a theology that sanctions legal separation, racial discrimination, and political disenfranchisement is not a true expression of the gospel. The task then of Christian theology is to expose that contradiction and to announce the good news of God's liberating reign to the world.

Moving forward, the task of the theologian is to convey God's disdain with the hijacking of a Christian faith that claims to represent God but in the end has only served as a pretext for white racism. Christian faith has been fashioned such that its sacred nature has been attached to Black dehumanization from the holds of ships to today. It has come to reverse God's and Jesus's identification with the oppressed by linking both to whiteness, which has been imperialistic, macabre, and demonic. It has been the best example of the Antichrist and not Christ. It has desecrated biblical revelation by maintaining that its essence is to condone human enslavement and Black enslavement to white people, in particular.

We must come to reimage Christian faith from its current practice so that it may be in spiritual oneness with the God of Jesus Christ. To do so, we must make right theologically what whites have made wrong. God sent Moses to Egypt for the *liberation* of the Israelites, not their continued enslavement. That means that the God of biblical revelation sides with the oppressed, not the oppressor. In our time that is Black people! Thus Black is beautiful, because it best symbolizes where God's liberating reign resides in contemporary times. Thus, the life of faith can no longer be lived in the absence of its liberation imperative. For it is that imperative that truly makes it the gospel. It can no longer be used as a front for normalizing

---

17. The words of a private white man from Maine, taken from Edward J. Blum and Paul Harvey, *The Color of Christ: The Son of God and the Saga of Race in America* (Chapel Hill, NC: University of North Carolina Press, 2012), 126.

human oppression. It can no longer be seen as complete as long as it is structured by rituals, frequent worship, the payment of tithes, and a strong prayer life. To do so is to continue to rob the gospel of its liberating foundation. To do so is to continue to impress upon converts that the gospel has nothing to do with human liberation, with the eradication of oppressive relationships, and that it is not principally concerned with those who suffer from those relationships. We must not continue to present the convert with an ill-informed and truncated gospel. Rather, its completeness is found in God's continual relationship with an oppressed people (Israel); God was so committed that God became Jesus to bring a new covenant into the world that identifies first and foremost with their suffering and the suffering that is sure to come in the struggle against oppressive forces in society. God comes in Jesus to bring the good news of the victory over that suffering through the cross and resurrection.

Jesus has not done it all for us while we simply celebrate his life two thousand years ago. The life of Jesus represents the struggle in our time as the forces of oppression respond violently and demonically as they did in Jesus's lifetime. This is exemplified in the old hymn of the church, "Just as there was a cross for Jesus, there is a cross for you and a cross for me!" Yet, remember that the promise of God, "I am with you always, to the end of the age" (Matt 28:20), resonates as an eternal covenant God made with oppressed humanity. God is there with Black people as a struggling co-partner fully identifying with the symbol of oppression itself—blackness! This is why James Cone proclaimed, "Black is holy, that is, it is a symbol of God's presence in history on behalf of the oppressed man."[18]

Consequently, the path of conversion impresses upon the convert the liberating foundation of the gospel as the central meaning of faith. That path also brings a prophetic critique of a theology devoid of socio-political liberation, and makes known the liberating meaning of the gospel. The path of conversion becomes authentic only when the falsehoods of racist Christianity are exposed and replaced with the truth of the liberating reign of God.

---

18. Cone, *Black Theology & Black Power*, 69.

3

The Path of Obedience

The God of Black liberation demands obedience to that God and that God alone. Yet, within the historical context of slavocracy, whites gave themselves the title of master. With that also came the process of justifying that slavocracy theologically. What better way to mentally control slaves than to convince them that the Word of God called for their eternal enslavement.

Paul's letter to the faithful at Ephesus became a favorite scripture for white Christian leadership to establish itself as an object of obedience. In the last chapter of the letter to the Ephesians, Paul provides instruction on two relationships. After relaying the proper deference for children regarding parents, Paul turns his attention to slaves and masters.

> Slaves, obey your earthly masters with fear and trembling, in singleness of heart, as you obey Christ; not only while being watched, and in order to please them, but as slaves of Christ, doing the will of God from the heart. Render service with enthusiasm, as to the Lord and not to men and women, knowing that whatever good we do, we will receive the same again from the Lord, whether we are slaves or free. (Eph 6:5–8)

Theologians agree that this is one of the most widely used biblical passages justifying Black subordination. On the surface, this seems an airtight pretext for Black obedience to white rule. But two points bear mentioning.

First, Paul's intent was not to justify human stratification as a demand of divine principle. Regardless of the categories of racial and religious life, the objective from the outset of Paul's ministry was to rid us of strict adherence to dogma and societal categories. Paul wanted us to get on with the task of living in a free society—a theme found also in Galatians. Void of any exacting criteria for what the ideal master–slave relationship should look like, I am sure Paul did not intend obedience to a master who called on slaves to accept their reduction to chattel, total disenfranchisement, and the violent dehumanization associated with the African slave trade. This is evident in the next two verses, where Paul instructs masters, "And, masters, do the same to them. Stop threatening them, for you know that both of you have the same Master in heaven, and with him there is no partiality" (vv. 9–10). Conveniently, these verses never made their way into the biblical hermeneutics of early colonial life. They affirm that God does not will one human group's complete surrender to another as a requirement for moral uprightness. Rather, God created all human beings in freedom, and where there is an oppressive relationship, God intervenes in history to bring that oppressive relationship to its demise.

Second, in neither of the above narratives is a future relationship of slavery—some sixteen hundred years later and in a different geographical area of the world—between European masters and West African slaves foreshadowed by Jesus or Paul. At best, we can say that Paul inherited a master–slave relationship from the Greco-Roman Empire and sought a future that was free from such relationships. We can also say that, in first-century Palestine, Paul also sought a society free from theological justifications for such relationships. As such, there is no biblical evidence that God actually revealed to Western Europeans that they should create a master–slave relationship with West Africans. From this narrative, there is no evidence that God declared African slavery eternal. Furthermore, the notion that the most important Christian duty was to "introduce" heathen Africans to the gospel is theologically and historically tenuous.[1]

---

1. West Africans were well aware of Christianity and practiced it long before the "introduction" to the faith by European Christian leadership in the slave trade. Biblical revelation itself sets the locale of many narra-

The real question at hand is what the God of Black liberation calls on the human family to do in a postslavery but not postracial society. That God would have us pursue a liberating obedience as a responsible co-partner with God seeking Black liberation. It is God's response to the ultimate question in contemporary America: How is obedience to be lived in a society in which whites continue to make the major political and theological decisions? The lessons of history have taught Black people of the continued deep-seated prejudices whereby racism mutates and breeds another form of Black obedience to white rule in every generation! From slavery to segregation to a racist criminal justice system to still highly disparate educational resources between whites and Blacks, each generation brings with it a new form of racial antagonism, despite pretensions to postracialism. And furthermore, the white Christian establishment has, for the most part, condoned these racial "transitions" through their silence on Black disenfranchisement. These religious "leaders" still cling to a porous understanding of separation of church and state that celebrates a deep fissure between institutional religion and societal transformation.

Obedience to God should never be equated with silence on issues of oppression; silence is tantamount to sanction! Obedience to God is an organic phenomenon geared toward bringing out the best in others as you demand that best for yourself. This is why obedience should never be equated with passive resignation, for Christian faith is proactive in defense of the downtrodden! As Gutiérrez reminds us, the gospel is still good news in the midst of suffering for "the least of these."

---

tives in Africa to include the Ethiopian eunuch baptized by Philip in Acts 8:26–40. We also saw the development of Coptic Christianity in northeast Africa and the formation of a distinctive West African Christianity long before the European invasion. Although it was the minority religion in terms of official adherents behind African Traditional Religions (ATR) and Islam, it exacted a strong presence in precolonial Africa. See John Mbiti, *African Religions and Philosophy*, 2nd ed. (Portsmouth, NH: Heinemann Books, 1990). See also Cheikh Anta Diop, *Precolonial Black Africa* (New York: Lawrence Hill Books, 1987).

> Skepticism and submissive resignation in the face of historical events are not Christian attitudes, because they take no account of hope. One of the tasks of the prophets was to feed the hopes of the people in times of crisis. This tradition was continued by the author of the Apocalypse, which is addressed to Christian communities that are bowed under the weight of persecution and of the death that the great empire of the day was entering.[2]

As Gutiérrez has struggled with this static obedience, so too have African Americans. As customs change over time, the human family must forever remain committed to the core principle of God—liberation! It is the task of the church to recognize these two poles of revelation—obedience and liberation—celebrate the inescapable tension inherent in these poles, and present a "new" theology that faithfully informs the oppressed in their struggle for freedom. The challenge of the church is to live by a hope that is rooted in the concrete history of a people who were at once oppressed and believing, and that is inspired by the plan of the kingdom, which urges us on to something new and different.[3] In our time, that identification goes to Black people, who still live in the same jurisdiction with the descendants of those who have stereotyped, mocked, and tortured them and who continually demand that Black people see their treatment as salvific. Devoid of a liberation imperative in white theology, true obedience calls for a complete demolition of the white privilege that still guides the contemporary scene. Only then will we heed the call by the God of Black liberation for "something new and different."

Christian Obedience in an Oppressed Context

For Black people, Christian obedience has been the biggest demand from the white Christian establishment. No moral precept gar-

---

2. Gustavo Gutiérrez, *The God of Life* (Maryknoll, NY: Orbis Books, 1991), 107.

3. Gutiérrez, *The God of Life*, 107.

nered more attention, and, more importantly, no *theological* precept garnered more attention. An obedient slave was not only a "good" slave, but, because of the connection to Christian morality, an obedient slave was engaged in God-pleasing behavior—the goal of any person of faith. Thus, Black people's first foray into Christian life involved obedience to their earthly masters. After a few generations of the slavocracy, Christian obedience had become the most formidable obstacle to a free Black humanity, and the white community had become thoroughly sold on the God-given source of slavery's origins.

> Besides the practice of white slave masters' Christianity, white theology sought to control and make black people slaves to its *doctrinal propositions*. The uncivilized witness and ethics of whites were not simply aberrations from their faith claims about God. On the contrary, white folks literally practiced what they preached. Their *theology* itself propagated white control and black subservience as the normative expression of the Christian gospel.[4]

The most ingenious way to put forward an ethic of obedience was to connect it to the divine will. As stated above, white Christian leadership sought an easy affinity between the Word of God and Black bondage, calling on slaves to "obey their masters." In short, white religious leadership was seeking a link between slavery in the Greco-Roman world and slavery in the American context. With that, white pastors took every opportunity—either in remarks or in sermons—to impress upon the slaves that the Bible ordained their enslavement; and, as such, it should not be challenged for to do so was to bring God's chastisement.

> First, the worship leader "always took his text from Ephesians, the white preacher did, the part what said, 'Obey

---

4. Dwight Hopkins, "Slave Theology in the Invisible Institution," in Dwight N. Hopkins and George C. L. Cummings, *Cut Loose Your Stammering Tongue: Black Theology in the Slave Narratives* (Maryknoll, NY: Orbis Books, 1991), 11.

your masters, be good servants.'" Hence, whites employed the authority of the Bible in a self-serving and racist interpretation. Having adopted this Pauline epistle as a standard homily, slave masters further construed a catechism for their black human property. "We had a catechism to learn . . . this wuz it: Be nice to massa an' missus, don't tell lies, don't be mean, be *obedient* an' work hard."[5]

Another frequently used catechism was:

> *Who gave you a master and a mistress?*
>   God gave them to me.
> *Who says that you must obey them?*
>   God says that I must.
> *What book tells you these things?*
>   The Bible.[6]

As an example of what would become the norm for white Christian leaders to engender complete dependence in slaves, this narrative from an ex-slave is representative of the time.

> Now I takes my text, which is, Nigger obey your master and your mistress, 'cause what you git from them here in this world am all you ever goin' to git, 'cause you just like the hogs and the other animals—when you dies, you ain't no more, after you been throwed in that hole.[7]

These maliciously cruel and demeaning statements were styled as the lot that God had cast for Blacks, and they were told that their fate would have been far worse if they had not been enslaved. Consequently, the hope (and I use that term with some trepidation) was to instill in slaves a resignation to their existence while having them understand their lot in a benevolent way. More importantly,

---

5. Hopkins and Cummings, *Cut Loose Your Stammering Tongue*, 11.
6. See Forrest G. Wood, *The Arrogance of Faith: Christianity & Race in America from the Colonial Era to the Twentieth Century* (Boston: Northeastern University Press, 1990), 72.
7. Hopkins and Cummings, *Cut Loose Your Stammering Tongue*, 11.

this homiletical prerogative by white ministers affirmed *whites as the mediators of God to be obeyed by Blacks as they demonstrated their obedience to God*. The theological reason for such preaching was to connect slave resignation to divine obedience. The secular reason, however, was to create an economic empire for whites without Blacks sharing in the fruits of its labor and to create complete Black dependence on whites.

By making themselves mediators between God and Blacks, whites sought to convince Blacks that they were the only path to salvation. This approach became more effective over generations as the slavocracy progressed and the remembrance of Africa faded and the imposition of white ideological indoctrination became more of a social mainstay in the colonies. In essence, slavery was regarded as the creation of God and not of white men. The sell was that whites were not distorting the gospel but simply living it faithfully in a postbiblical era. Thus, if slaves wanted a faithful relationship with God, obedience meant the unconditional surrender of mind, body, and spirit to their "earthly" masters. This meant that the path of obedience for Blacks could come only through white theological guidance or, in other words, that "white men are the way, the truth, and the life . . . no one comes to God except through white men!" In reality, this meant Blacks accepting a subordinate status and everything that came with it! The dehumanizing acts by white slaveholders were meant to demonstrate that God had carved out a path of obedience that entailed rapes, whippings, floggings, castrations, and later lynchings of Black people that were cruel but necessary to keep Blacks from rebelling against God's eternal will. In a similar context, in his provocative 1894 work, *The Kingdom of God Is within You*, Leo Tolstoy offers the same rationale for violence against Russian peasants, even after they had surrendered during a revolt.

> When I inquired of one of the governors why they made use of this kind of torture when people had already submitted and soldiers were stationed in the village, he replied with the important air of a man who thoroughly understands

all the subtleties of statecraft, that if the peasants were not thoroughly subdued by flogging, they would begin offering opposition to the decisions of authorities again. When some of them had been thoroughly tortured, the authority of the state would be secured forever among them.[8]

Thus, the process of impressing upon subjects the eternal nature of their "station" in life becomes a staple part of maintaining oppressive authority. But more significantly, complete capitulation to "earthly" authority is the end goal until the eschaton. It was by precisely the same means, that is, through murder and torture, that *obedience* to the decisions of higher authorities was to be secured.[9]

The God of Black liberation, however, calls us to a different form of faithfulness. Slavery's end should make clear that the will of God is liberation and not oppression. To do otherwise is to contradict God's creative intent.[10] The theological rationale offered by white theologians is that Black people's rebellion is what ended the slavocracy without the vision to see that it is the God of Black liberation that has inspired Black people to revolt against racist hegemony from the outset of their bondage. This is the very reason why human tyranny in any form is ultimately defeated. The God of Black liberation's nature cosmically reflects God's will historically. In other words, God's creation in freedom, and specifically of humans in freedom, is a direct reflection of God's nature. In this sense, God does not create slaves, humans do; and humans do not strike the first blow for freedom, God does! Thus, God stands in diametric opposition to any context of bondage and instills in the oppressed group the incessant restlessness for freedom. Even at the point of enduring the complete repertoire of white torture, Black

---

8. Leo Tolstoy, *The Kingdom of God Is within You* (Lincoln, NE: University of Nebraska Press, 1984), 288.

9. Tolstoy, *The Kingdom of God Is within You*, 288.

10. Even the human family's demarcation into racial groups is a contradiction to God's creative intent. See Ashley Montague's classic treatment of the dubious process of racial categorization, *Man's Most Dangerous Myth: The Fallacy of Race* (Lanham, MA: Alta Mira Press, 1997).

restlessness with bondage was never destroyed, given that it is as eternal as its source. To this end, God does not sanction a hierarchical relationship between human groups but does intervene for its dissolution.

God heard Israel's cries in Egypt and did not decide on inactivity but rather called Moses to send the Israelites out of Egypt and Pharaoh's army to the Red Sea. Thus, the liberation imperative of God for the oppressed, even with some Israelites desiring to stay with Pharaoh, is a nonnegotiable demand. In other words, God is not a God of human oppression but a God of human liberation. It also means that oppression in any form is a product of an avaricious mind, not a product of divine intent. The same concern for human freedom is exemplified in the pronouncements of divine chastisement by the prophets as they confronted contexts of human oppression. Amos called for justice and righteousness and not for "the noise of solemn assemblies" (Amos 5:21–24). Micah called for justice, kindness, and humility (Micah 6:8); and Joel announced a gathering into the valley of Jehoshaphat (Hebrew for the place of judgment) for those who had dehumanized Israel by "scattering them among other nations and dividing up their land" (Joel 3:2). And as we saw in the first chapter, God came in Jesus to announce to the world that we all now have the freedom to pursue freedom. That is the meaning of the new covenant. Thus, distorting the gospel to justify human domination does not earn one the love of God but rather the chastisement of God.

That same chastisement holds true for America as well. Black revolutionary and author David Walker takes umbrage with a section of Thomas Jefferson's *Notes on the State of Virginia* in which Jefferson takes straight aim at the aesthetic and cultural features of Black people when he maintained that "[Blacks] whether originally a distinct race, or made distinct by time and circumstances, are *inferior* to the whites in the endowments of body and mind" and that, "this *unfortunate* difference of colour and *perhaps of faculty*, is a powerful obstacle to the emancipation of these people." Furthermore, Jefferson questioned the equal human worth of Blacks when he wrote, "Many of their advocates, while they wish to vindicate the liberty of human nature are anxious also to preserve its *dignity* and *beauty*." But Walker signals the era of a new way of Christian obedience by calling slaves to the task of bringing the slavocracy to its knees and abandoning the distorted gospel of Christian submission.

> Now I ask you candidly, my suffering brethren in time, who are candidates of the eternal worlds, how could Mr. Jefferson but have given the world these remarks respecting us, when we are so submissive to them, and so much servile deceit prevail among ourselves—when we so meanly submit their murderous lashes, to which neither the Indians nor any other people under Heaven would submit? No, they would die to a man, before they would suffer such things from men who are no better than themselves, and *perhaps not so good*.[11]

Walker sought to instill a freedom or death mentality in Black people not simply as a historical solution to the racial problem but as the wrath of God intervening in history on behalf of oppressed Blacks, assuring them that rebelling to end their bondage is synonymous with God's will. He writes,

> When I reflect that God is just, and that millions of my wretched brethren would meet death with glory—yea, more, would plunge into the very mouth of cannons and be torn into particles as minute as the atoms which compose the elements of the earth, in preference to a mean submission to the lash of tyrants, I am with streaming eyes, compelled to shrink back into nothingness before my Maker, and exclaim again, thy will be done, O Lord God Almighty.[12]

Walker is establishing the theological imperative, as all the great freedom fighters have, that Christian obedience is not synonymous with Black enslavement. It subverts God's intention

---

11. David Walker, *The Appeal to the Coloured Citizens of the World* (Baltimore, MD: Black Classic Press, 1993; orig., 1830), 47.
12. Walker, *The Appeal to the Coloured Citizens of the World*, 48.

for humanity and compromises the Black psyche to see itself in the image of God. Christian obedience is not rooted in human oppression but in human liberation. Jesus's atoning death and resurrection have made God's intention known to humanity that obedience no longer needs a human mediator, let alone a mediator who is obsessed with pretensions of his superiority. On the contrary, Christian obedience frees the oppressed, in this case Black people, to pursue their freedom no longer bound by the static categories of the Greco-Roman world that Paul inherited or the racist Christian anthropology of white theologians against whom Black people continue to struggle. The God of Black liberation requires obedience to that God and that God alone—for liberation, not oppression! The most significant way in which the Protestant Reformation informed the Black liberation struggle is that it removed an official mediator, even in ministerial form, from the equation of striking decisive blows for freedom. The God of Black liberation is concerned only with the liberating mediator who answers the genuine call to set the captives free. Christian obedience is not to be measured by "obeying" the call to view protest as ungodly or by measuring the Christian life by interior well-being. Those are the musings of a white preacher and not God! Rather the God of Black liberation acts in human history and is constantly at work freeing Black people of their mental and cultural attachment to whiteness and frees them to endure whatever white obstacles present themselves along the journey to freedom. In short, Christian obedience is to be measured by obeying God's command to be a liberated people. In so doing, we will create a world that truly reflects God's nature.

Obedience to God and Human Liberation

What is needed is an obedience wherein divine freedom does not reduce Black humanity to chattel or second-class citizens. In other words, obedience to God is no longer synonymous with obedience to white pronouncements of eternal oppression and heaven for "good" behavior on earth. For whites, good Black behavior has always meant a complete surrender to white rule! Essentially, this meant that since white Christian leadership was not going to relent in its distorted theology of Black dehumanization, it had to be eliminated as a mediator. White theology and the white segregated church could never give the answers to the urgent theological questions of Black people, simply because these questions could not even be asked.[13] A new theological method had to be born that takes the white theological model of the religious individual over issues of human liberation and stands it on its head, that is, issues of human liberation now have to take precedence over the religious individual and otherworldliness. Presbyterian minister and freedom fighter Henry Highland Garnet makes this new theological method clear.

> The divine commandments you are duty bound to reverence and obey. If you do not obey them, you will surely meet with the displeasure of the Almighty. He requires you to love Him supremely, and your neighbor as yourself—to keep the Sabbath Day Holy—to search the Scriptures—and bring up your children with respect to His laws, and to worship no other God but Him. But slavery sets all these at naught, and hurls defiance in the face of Jehovah. The forlorn condition in which you are placed does not destroy your obligation to God. You are not certain of heaven, because you allow yourselves to remain in a state of slavery, where you cannot obey the commandments of the Sovereign of the universe.[14]

Garnet makes clear that in a "normal" or noncolonial setting, keeping the commandments as instructed by biblical revelation

---

13. Allen Aubrey Boesak, *Farewell to Innocence: A Socio-Ethical Study on Black Theology and Black Power* (Maryknoll, NY: Orbis Books, 1976), 38.

14. Carter G. Woodson, *Negro Orators and Their Orations* (Washington, DC: Associated Publishers, 1925); taken from Mays, *The Negro's God* (Westport, CT: Greenwood Publishing, 1969; orig., 1938), 46.

is the best, if not the only, path to obedience. Yet, Garnet is also clear that in a colonial setting, such as the one in which Black folks find themselves, obedience to God calls for a reversal of the commandments. Or as Garnet stated, "slavery brings all these at naught." This means that a new treatment of obedience had to be constructed that gives primacy to the struggle to end Black suffering before all else.

> Man was created in the image of God and as such has infinite worth and dignity. Therefore, slavery and obedience to God are two things that cannot be reconciled. Slavery is not only subservience; it is also idolatry.[15]

Garnet, like most freedom fighters, was well aware that slavery had a direct impact on a community's ability to keep the commandments. As long as Black people remained in a "forlorn condition," keeping the commandments was in itself an impossible task and ultimately a red herring, keeping the attention of Black people on being "good" for white folks and focused on the relief of a heaven that may or may not exist after physical death. Moreover, Garnet understood that the path of obedience was paved with freedom guiding it and that to lose sight of that base was to lose sight of God. Therefore, to return Black people back to their original state of freedom in God, ending institutional racism must serve as the theological point of departure. As Mays noted,

> Garnet, like most of his predecessors since 1760, saw one outstanding need for his people—freedom from the curse and thralldom of slavery. He, like others, felt there could be no kind of status and no security for the race without complete release from bondage. Security and status in freedom were sought mainly in this world. Some of these men developed the idea of God to persuade the masters to free the slaves because slavery was against God, but others urged a more violent way of freeing slaves, arguing that God would

---

15. Words of Garnet; see Boesak, *Farewell to Innocence*, 40.

smile upon the slaves' efforts if they would strike a blow for freedom.[16]

Garnet brings two dimensions to our discussion that remain operative today. First, he inverts the eschatological treatment of white Christian ministers who maintained that status and freedom should be sought in heaven and not this world. Garnet opts instead for the ultimate significance of the affairs of this world—a world of hell for Black people that the God of Jesus Christ demands to be liberated. Thus, the divine commandment of freedom now trumps all other commandments with the assurance that, through the death and resurrection of Jesus, eradicating oppression, here and now, is of the greatest significance to God. Second, the path of obedience demands that the greatest commandment is no longer keeping the sabbath holy and loving your neighbor as yourself but ending Black oppression. Divine obedience to ending Black oppression does indeed place the community in sync with the God of Black liberation. While the most effective methodology has been a subject of intense dialogue in the life of the Black community, one constant reigns supreme—the God of Black liberation smiles on Black people when they strike a blow for freedom. This is the understanding of faith from the ancestors who knew that the white church was a theological sham and sought the far more strategic confines of the brush arbors to communicate with the God of Black liberation—a God who had revealed to them the morally bankrupt nature of their condition. They were fully aware that the God who had demanded their devotion and the Spirit who infused their secret meetings and possessed their souls and bodies in the ecstasy of worship was not the God of the slave master with his whip and gun, nor the God of the plantation preacher with his segregated services and unctuous injunction to humility and *obedience*.[17]

---

16. Mays, *The Negro's God*, 47.

17. Words of Gayraud S. Wilmore; see Boesak, *Farewell to Innocence*, 37–38.

To be sure, the debate has centered around whether the movement from oppression to liberation should be violent or nonviolent, especially in the face of the persistent violence that both white civilians and white law enforcement have heaped on Black people. Yet, what has remained a mainstay in the annals of Black struggle has been the summary adoption that a blow for freedom had to be administered . . . again and again! For example, while Nat Turner represented a freedom that was violent, Martin Luther King Jr. represented a freedom that was nonviolent; and yet both men were eventually assassinated through white violence! Both men were ministers and men of God who rightly understood the divine call to liberation and dedicated their ministries to inverting the white way of life in America—and that meant eliminating white preachers as mediators. They were men of God who heeded the call to the base of the cross as Paul heeded the Macedonian call on the road to Damascus.

The God of Black liberation calls for an obedience in divine freedom even as the institution of slavery has been defeated; but structural injustice still prevails racially, and Black people are still subject to systemic bigotry and random acts of violence at any time. Paul's Macedonian call should still be the rallying cry, and divine obedience should be measured by the concrete response to racist aggression. The encounter of God's liberating presence includes hearing the call to be obedient to the claim of divine freedom. As James Cone noted, Christian behavior is essentially the behavior that arises out of the oppressed community in response to God's call to be obedient to his (God's) will.[18] Cone takes the baton from Garnet. He is warning the community not to fall prey to interior blessings as the foundation of all God-talk. Rather, we must understand that Black people's love affair with a God of personal blessings is a white ruse and limits the Black community's power to free itself from white control. In like manner, Black

---

18. James H. Cone, *God of the Oppressed* (Maryknoll, NY: Orbis Books, 1997), 207.

people's love affair with a God of heaven after death is a product of a white racist mind created to make contented "Negroes" but not free human beings. Such a view of God is fraudulent inasmuch as it depicts the God of biblical revelation as the mastermind of white superiority.

Importantly, Cone is throwing down the gauntlet here by linking obedience to God with divine encounter. For him, no one can claim an authentic encounter with God and at the same time champion Black oppression or live in passive resignation to it. Rather, the authentic encounter with God brings one to the intersection of oppression and liberation. In other words, the authentic encounter with God mandates a Christian behavior "that arises out of an oppressed community." This means that Christian obedience is the commitment to move an oppressed community to its God-appointed liberation; any other activity in God's name ceases to be Christian obedience. It also means that human history—not heaven—is the venue where God intervenes on behalf of the oppressed to make God's unconditional will for liberation known. We know God's will by virtue of God's consistent intervention on behalf of the lowly and the despised, making the struggle of the oppressed God's struggle.

> God enters into a social context of oppression and liberates the people into a new existence. At the precise moment that divine liberation happens, a divine claim is laid upon the oppressed to be what God has made them.[19]

And from creation God has made them free, and that frees them to rebel against their condition. Thus, in an oppressed context, God inverts religious custom by ending our attachment to the "divine commandments" and frees us to set our theological sights on *the* commandment of human liberation. For how is one to immerse oneself in the universals of loving your neighbor as yourself or keeping the sabbath holy or, for our times, making sure you have a church home, a strong prayer life, and that tithes are

---

19. Cone, *God of the Oppressed*, 207.

regularly paid in a context of such macabre inhumanity directed toward Black people? How is one to value ritual and otherworldliness over socio-political liberation in a context of Black oppression? How is one, in the words of David, the psalmist, to sing the songs of the Lord in a strange land? (cf. Ps 137:4)—a land that has been as hostile as it has been strange; a land that has shown no signs of repenting for its racist behavior but has strategically regrouped in every generation, making the struggle for true Christian obedience just as crucial today as it was in the nineteenth century. This means that the struggle for a true obedience in blackness must be the only point of departure for a people still struggling for freedom and self-determination. Obedience to God must be the eternal home for Black people, not white theologians. This involves a new way of being religious that does not emerge out of personalism and homophobia, which are the diversions of white Christianity. It means a new way of being theological that affirms blackness as the point of departure for relevant discourse independent of white thought. This, admittedly, is a tall order but a necessary one in a nation where a theological inversion is the key to its salvation. Invariably, if Black people leave their liberation to white Christian leaders, they will keep Black people mired in a theology of white privilege and of a racist status quo, reminding them of the dangers of change that is too fast or too soon. They will keep Black people mired in quaint Bible studies where they dictate the terms of discourse that are usually centered around the goodness of the Lord and universal references to God's love for all humans and certainly to biblical inerrancy, while giving no attention to the system of racial caste from which they continually benefit. We need a Christian obedience that is unreservedly rooted in Black liberation, and that means a new way of being Christian. In this respect, Cone notes,

> Obedience always means going where we otherwise would not go; being what we would not be; doing what we would not do. Reconciliation means that Christ has freed us for this. In a white racist society, Christian obedience can only

mean being obedient to blackness, its glorification and exaltation.[20]

Black people have tried the white way of life, but it has not recognized Black people as equals. Black people have also tried white theology, but that has a problem identifying the liberation imperative inherent in the gospel—both the white way of life and white theology are inescapably racist. To put it in eschatological terms: a white man's heaven has been Black people's hell!

An authentic encounter with God cannot be found in the confines of traditional Christian obedience. It is white and it is racist! Thus, the white mediator must be eliminated. In a context of Black oppression, the true encounter with God recognizes God's exclusive commitment to human liberation—nothing more; nothing less!

Obedience, Black Liberation, and the Life of Jesus

The God of Black liberation calls for a Christian obedience that has the courage to challenge preexisting patterns of orthodoxy and forges the path of obedience to a liberating worldview. This involves conflicts with existing structures that insist on a racist status quo. In other words, obedience to God calls for a new way of being religious that advocates for the masses with the goal "to make the last, first." Such an example is found in the life of Jesus.

Jesus's ministry was mired in constant conflict and represented God's will for the new Jerusalem—a new world that calls for a transformation of the current way of viewing and living in the world. As Albert Cleage notes,

> The whole life of Jesus was a life of conflict. If we reject conflict, then we must find a Messiah who did not deal in conflict. Jesus was in constant opposition to the established power structure. The course of his ministry was determined

---

20. James H. Cone, *Black Theology & Black Power* (Maryknoll, NY: Orbis Books, 1989), 150–51.

by his flights to avoid assassination. Jesus was a threat to the establishment.[21]

The source of that conflict was the threat Jesus brought to the political and religious leaders of his time—those who were content with the existing situation and were willing to do anything to preserve it—*even, as it turned out, kill God*! Thus, Christian obedience came to be understood as a commitment to carry out character, spiritual, and physical assassination in order to maintain racial privilege and not as a commitment to raze the foundations of racial privilege. In the parable of the good Samaritan (Luke 10:25–37), the scribe seeks to assassinate the character of Jesus when he asks Jesus, "Who is my neighbor?" The intent here was to humiliate Jesus publicly; but in his response, Jesus tells the scribe that it was not the priest or the Levite—the established religious leadership of the time—who stopped and helped the man in his bludgeoned condition, rather it was a person from a despised community—the Samaritans—who helped the man in need. Certainly, Jesus was inaugurating a new era in which one's neighbor was no longer defined by spatial location but by the ability to see the inherent equal worth of every human being. It was clearly Jesus's way of empowering the Samaritan community in a society that had devalued them for no other reason than their nationality, in a manner similar to Black people's vilification by the white power structure.

In an example of acute spiritual assassination, Jesus was out healing a blind man when the religious leaders of his time, driven by traditional custom, thought he should have been in the temple worshiping. They wanted the man to give Jesus up or to castigate him for claiming to have healing powers. They even offered an epitaph to the man to describe Jesus as a sinner! Yet, not only did the blind man not give Jesus up, he answered in precisely the manner in which Jesus desired. The blind man referred to his newfound sight and not Jesus's character when he responded, "I do not know

---

21. Albert B. Cleage Jr., *Black Christian Nationalism: New Directions for the Black Church* (New York: William Morrow, 1972), 182.

whether he is a sinner. One thing I do know, that though I was blind, now I see" (John 9:25). Their desire to see Jesus branded as a sinner and a con man had been publicly rebuffed not by Jesus but by the one whom he had healed. Such have been the castigations of the white establishment about Black leaders who have agitated for justice . . . to get the Black masses to denounce their public impact as sinful, ungodly, and un-Christian or just not good for America!

Ultimately, when Jesus's ministry was having too much of a liberating impact on the masses, the chief priests and elders—the religious establishment, along with District Attorney Pilate—decided that the time had come for Jesus to be physically assassinated. Jesus was then arrested and brought to trial after that same establishment convinced Judas to give up Jesus's location. The plan was to convict him for treason, but they had no evidence. However, because his work made his own people feel uncomfortable due to the stereotypes they had internalized about legitimate leadership, they gave up Jesus to Pilate for Barabbas, a common criminal, and sentenced Jesus to the capital punishment of that time—crucifixion. Thus, God had come into the world to bring a new covenant, but because the religious leadership was so deeply entrenched in their "old" ways, they sent God to death on the cross (Matt 27:1–26).

All three of these biblical narratives demonstrate not only that the despised community is valued but also that the salvation of humanity is bound up in its liberation, the meaning of the Christ event. This is the essence of God's message to the world in Jesus. Through the life of Jesus, God demonstrates his love for freedom through his identification with the despised in their struggle for self-determination. Jesus's message to the world was that the old, traditional way of being human had outlived its usefulness, and the advent of the new covenant was upon us. The good news is that God had come to show the world that stereotyping communities on the basis of race no longer had any place in God's kingdom. The perpetuation of centuries-old religious patterns that either sanctioned or ignored human oppression has no place in the world. The world was finally faced with God incarnate. God came in Jesus to proclaim to the world that the old covenant rooted in claims of human superiority was not Christ-like but was the Antichrist. Thus, obedience to God in an oppressive world will end at the cross for those fighting for human liberation. Obedience to God is the negation of obedience to human oppression—and that means conflict.

> Any liberation struggle must involve confrontation and conflict. There is no such thing as a peaceful, calm, quiet, liberation struggle. Even Dr. King's nonviolent phase of our liberation struggle involved conflict. Every time he went into a city and organized a mass demonstration and brought black folks out to protest in the streets, white people confronted them and there was conflict. The fact that they kept marching and protesting day after day made it conflict in spite of the fact that they did not strike back.[22]

In summing up these biblical narratives, Cleage notes that the road to liberation entails confronting, not coddling, bigoted leaders. It means confronting the evil in the world that keeps the masses from being free and being a voice for their freedom. We must come to learn that with Jesus there can be no obedience to God without conflict, and there can be no human liberation without struggle unto death. As Cone rightly notes,

> For Christians, Jesus is the source for what we do; without his power to make life human, our behavior would count as nothing. For Jesus is the ethical criterion of our judgment.[23]

But the scandal of the gospel is that contemporary freedom fighters must be ready to contextualize the gospel out of its oppressive trappings, knowing that we have the power through Jesus's resurrection to demonstrate Christian obedience by bringing God's liberating reign to the Black liberation struggle.

---

22. Cleage Jr., *Black Christian Nationalism*, 182.
23. Cone, *God of the Oppressed*, 208.

> We do not simply ask: "What would Jesus do?" as if he is an ethical principle to be applied without the risk of faith. We ask, "What is he doing *now* in America and elsewhere to heal the sick and to liberate the prisoners?"[24]

Certainly, there will be Christians, both Black and white, who will find this question problematic. For them, the gospel is historic faith about Jesus healing individuals of infirmities in the first century. But this question is the challenge of the time—the challenge of the new covenant! Christian obedience is not just restricted to the personal realm and to the faithful calling on Jesus to perform a miracle twenty centuries later. If the incarnation is real, then it must be relevant! And the only way for it to be relevant in our time is to plunge it into the Black condition to bring life where racial bigotry has spawned death spiritually and physically.

Spiritual death has come through the imposition of white supremacy, the apparent approval of it by the white church, and the creation of "independent" Black churches not to bring Blacks closer to God but to make them better laborers. This should certainly lend itself to a jaundiced view of religion, when combined with the teaching that heaven is the only freedom a Black person could experience. In many ways, this is why, today, so many people who grew up in the church are disillusioned with organized religion. Indeed, this is a faith expression in which they should be disillusioned, if not enraged. But the good news of the gospel does not keep us mired in the dungeons of oppressive religion. Rather, it offers the promise that even spiritual death can be overcome through the resurrecting power of Jesus. Through his example of conflict with the authorities of his day, the power lies not in the death of the body but in the life of the spirit to defeat the oppressive powers of this world. The strength of obedience, then, lies not in summary agreement with popular religion but in embracing the new covenant of human liberation not bound by socially irrelevant structures.

---

24. Cone, *God of the Oppressed*, 208.

That is why the reconciling work of Jesus Christ involves a gathering of those who are committed to obedience in the world. The Christian community is inseparable from the work of the Holy Spirit. It is that community which accepts God's justification of man in Christ and is thus prepared to live as justified men.[25]

This involves humans who are prepared to live as the power of God in conflict with a racist status quo.

Physical death has come through an outright assault on Black skin. The well-documented horrors of holds of ships, auctions, floggings, rapes, lynchings, castrations, "scholarly" works like Charles Carroll's *The Negro: A Beast*, and Thomas Dixon's *The Leopard's Spots*, cinematic denunciations seen in D. W. Griffith's *The Birth of a Nation*, and the televised racist hyperbole of Black aesthetic features such as Stepin Fetchit, Mantan Moreland, and *Amos 'n' Andy* all sought to denigrate Black people and reduce them in the eyes of both white and Black people as a pitiable people, desperate for a more intelligent and clearly superior culture—white culture! No people have had their aesthetic features mocked more than Black people. No people have had their culture publicly ridiculed and misunderstood more than Black people. And no other people have had as many horrific tracts written about them and have been the butt of white jokes about their animalistic physical appearance and diminished intellectual endowment as Black people.

To engage in such racial chicanery, however, is to do the work of the Antichrist. To depict fellow human beings with such ill-will and blatant hatred is to desecrate the *imago dei* and to mock God for the way Black people have been created. More importantly, to ground the gospel in white privilege that aids and abets the mockery of Black humanity betrays the wisdom of God and is the height of sinfulness. But the good news of the gospel conveys to Black people that they are not and never were what white people said they were. It is not the white racist mediator but the direct link to

---

25. Cone, *Black Theology & Black Power*, 149.

God that grounds Black people in the work of engendering a more positive self-image and allows them to fall in love with, not hate, their blackness. It is God reconciling Godself with the despised and humiliated in the now-ness of human history. As Cone states,

> When we analyze the black-white relationship in the twentieth century in the light of God's reconciling work in Jesus Christ, the message is clear. For black people, it means God has reconciled us to an acceptance of blackness. If the death-resurrection of Christ means anything, it means that the blackness of black people is a creation of God himself. God came into the world in order that black people need not be ashamed of who they are. In Christ, we not only know who we are, but who God is.[26]

This is why obedience can never be equated with passive resignation to white directives about the gospel or Black humanity for that matter. The white Christian establishment is interested only in reconciling Blacks to whiteness, which is inherently racist. But it is God, through the death and resurrection of Jesus, who has reconciled Blacks to God. Buoyed by the resurrection, the struggle for Black liberation now hinges on Blacks falling in love with their blackness and burying white stereotypes about Black humanity in the cemetery of racial bigotry. Thus, the goodness of God lies not in the insanity of accepting white denunciations of Black humanity but in freeing Blacks to love their beautiful Black selves and to take on whatever comes in the way of white backlash in the process.

---

26. Cone, *Black Theology & Black Power*, 149.

4

The Path of Righteousness

The path of righteousness tells us to "strive first for the kingdom of God and his righteousness, and all these things will be given to you as well" (Matt 6:33). Yet, almost immediately, we fall into theological manipulation. Given that the kingdom has been associated more in Christian theology with heavenly reward than earthly birthright, the implication is that to seek righteousness is to seek the kingdom of heaven. But this has been the most seductive ruse of white theology as the kingdom of heaven has been shrouded in ideology from the inception of the colonies. Heaven was not a historical reality to be realized on earth, as it was taught to Black people, but a spirit-oriented place, spatial or not, that Blacks could only ascend to after physical death. The quid pro quo was that the kingdom of heaven was achieved only if the slave was "good" on earth. In other words, if the slave did not steal or run away from the plantation, performed the required daily goals of labor, and, of course, informed the master of any impending insurrection, then that slave was considered "good." More importantly, that slave was considered righteous. Essentially, the white Christian establishment made the measuring stick of righteousness a state of subordination for Blacks and, ultimately, for them to see that subordination is the key to their salvation.

Meanwhile, whites were using the (still uncompensated) slave labor of Blacks to create a heaven for themselves on earth, and they still enjoy the fruits of that privilege today. Barring the Civil War and the *Brown v. Board of Education* decision, American life has been a heaven on earth for whites. The hypocrisy is that white Christian leaders have consistently taught that heaven is an otherworldly, not an earthly, phenomenon. And therein lies the ideological rub. Heaven and the kingdom have been intrinsically connected to righteousness such that it has been used to make white privilege synonymous with the divine will. In other words, God's desire for racial relationships—white privilege—was and is unfolding in human history as God envisioned. This, however, is precisely why any liberating understanding of righteousness can no longer be linked to this theological structure. No theological method can be justified while it is demanding a group of humans to assume a subordinate status, even with the promise of heaven after death. Not only is it hypocritical; it is racist!

The God of Black liberation calls the human family to measure righteousness not by white dominance over Black people but by freedom from that distorted treatment of righteousness. Thus, to speak of the righteousness of God in a context of racial oppression is to speak of God's activity on behalf of Blacks and the punishment of their tormentors. God's righteousness is to be measured, first and foremost, not by unquestioned adherence to brutal repression nor to dogma and/or ritual but by God's justice on behalf of the despised.

Martin Luther raised the question regarding God's righteousness, What is meant by the justice of God? But his answers remained mired in the life of the institutional church. God's justice is less concerned about the church as a building of bricks and mortar and more concerned about the church's role in realizing a liberated world beyond church walls! This is the new covenant. Church is no longer a center for personal righteousness but the *vehicle* for human liberation. It is no longer a center for affirming a paralyzing self-righteousness but the opportunity to participate in the new covenant's demand of liberation for the oppressed. While Luther was correct that the justice of God should not cause us to fear and dread judgment day, especially about unknown sins, we need a broader conception of divine righteousness that extends to human oppression in the here and now. In other words, God's righteousness is not just an ecclesiastical phenomenon but a communal phenomenon; not just a Christian but a human phenomenon; not just a static but a transformative phenomenon. As Paul writes, "You were taught to put away your former way of life, your old self, corrupt and deluded by its lusts, and to be renewed in the spirit of your minds, and to clothe yourselves with the new self, created according to the likeness of God in true righteousness and holiness" (Eph 4:22–24).

Paul advocates an authentic righteousness that does not validate the status quo but is ever calling us to a new way of being human. Since the old (and current) way is one of acute privilege of one group over another—of the white over the Black, of the man over the woman, of the rich over the poor—we are compelled by God to redefine righteousness. We must bury the "old self," mentally and spiritually damaged by human oppression, and become the opposite. Righteousness can never be realized as long as one group is experiencing heaven at the expense of others; for, indeed, the privileged group is also not experiencing heaven. Since they are constantly in the throes of insecurity, incessantly working to beat back the dominated class's attempts to free themselves, the dominant class's heaven is but a mirage, an eschatological phantasm.

To be truly righteous, we must put on the new self by completely discarding the old self. That means whites putting down their bigoted ways or facing God's wrath. It means Blacks not "turning the other cheek" in the face of white encroachments but exposing insidious racism wherever it rears its head. Only then will we be "created to be like God" and return to the state in which God created us—truly free. God is not the God of white oppression but the God of Black liberation, given that blackness best represents what it is like to be oppressed. Righteousness has never consisted in a kingdom of heaven for one race and a kingdom of hell for another. There is no righteousness in a hell on earth for any of God's children. Rather, true righteousness must be measured by a heavenly state for all humans and not just the privileged. The process of creating privilege is in itself unrighteous, and the process of maintaining that privilege is even more unrighteous. In fact, any attempts to use Christian faith to bring legitimacy to an unrighteous cause is not only unrighteous but sinful!

To "strive first for the kingdom of God and his righteousness" means charting a new way of being righteous that identifies with the cause of the oppressed. It means compensating Black people for the indispensable labor in the building of this country. It means liberating the people who have been subject to close to six decades of "legal" separation. It means reforming a society in which white law enforcement officers or "conscientious civilians" continually gun down Black men with no regard to the sanctity of Black lives. It means ending the pitch to garner Black voters with the question: What do *you* people have to lose? For what has been legal to America has been illegal to God. The law of God does not entail creating contexts of human oppression and certainly does not mean using God's name to give them salvific import. Rather, this new way of being righteous means working for a heaven on earth that is not grounded in racial superiority. The God of Black liberation has charted a path of righteousness that frees the oppressed from earthly hell. Given that the God of creation is also the God of freedom, and given that we live in a context of oppression of Black people for no other reason than their blackness, the new way of being human—the new way to righteousness—must be found in God's blackness. Just as God identified with oppressed Israel in first-century Palestine, God similarly chooses liberation in this context of Black oppression for Black people. For only in that God, the God of the Black Christ, does the world find a true kingdom and a true righteousness.

The God of Social Righteousness

Insofar as the God of righteousness comes to realize heaven in this world by changing the socio-political plight of Black people, God has revealed Godself in the social context of Black oppression. In this sense, *the God of Black liberation comes to us as a God of social righteousness*. This is a nonnegotiable dimension of any treatment of righteousness, given the predominant distorted understanding of righteousness that has characterized Christian theology and furthers the cause of white supremacy. The social realm of human existence, by church decree, for far too long, has extended beyond the reach of divine righteousness. Human history remains an unquestioned training ground for both Black and white churches in forming adherents not in the way that God would have it but in the way that the white Christian establishment would have it, that is, a kingdom of white privilege. The kingdom of heaven they are seeking first is one devoid of racial equality—which is really no kingdom at all.

This approach to righteousness is unacceptable to the God of Black liberation, given its theological connectedness with human oppression. It was God's servant Job who, in the midst of acute suffering, offered us a righteousness on a higher plane: "Out of the north comes golden splendor; around God is awesome majesty. The Almighty—we cannot find him; he is great in power and justice, and abundant righteousness he will not violate" (Job 37:22–23). This passage has two implications on our path of righteousness. First, God is described as coming "out of the north" and as "great in power." Both quotes imply that although God intervenes in history on the side of the oppressed, God is not bound by history. "North" in this sense is not geographical but cosmic. God's northern habitat makes God different from anything "below," or rather, unable to be persuaded by the forces of racial imperialism to abandon the struggle for freedom. This was a highly galvanizing confirmation for a Black community in which all the earthly paths to freedom ended with a white blockade, particularly before the advent of the Underground Railroad. This understanding of God's "northern" reality also meant that the liberating plan for Black humanity could not be foiled by an Uncle Tom who subverted insurrections like those of Nat Turner or Denmark Vesey by disclosing them to white planters. With the God of Black liberation intervening from the "north" on behalf of Black people, white posses, along with their hunting dogs, could hang or lynch Black people, but they could not hang or lynch God. As a result, they did not possess the power to stop the Black freedom movement. This is what Job means by God as "great in power." It was a power that could not be compromised by racist forces. This empowered Black people to fight on against inhumane treatment, knowing that there was a power that could not be killed by the white power structure. Although Black people understood their mortality, their sense of destiny—the movement from bondage to freedom—was evident in their relationship with the God who was enabling them to sacrifice those mortal lives for the immortality of God's liberating reign. They were no longer bound by the pervasive reach of white power but were now living under the reign of a God who not only heard their cries but was committed to ending those cries. The most potent phenomenon in human history, white racism, had met its match—a God who transcended history, not in a glorification of escapism but in a liberating intervention to end Black oppression. Thus, Job makes clear that God is more powerful than any earthly system of injustice. God will stand the test of time against it. This is the justice of God.

Second, Job leaves no doubt as to the nature of God. He refers to God as one who "does not oppress." In so doing, Job nullifies any attempt on the part of a community's religious leaders to use God as a pretext for "kingdomizing" human oppression. He also nullifies any attempt to equate such "kingdomizing" with a greater good for the oppressed over several generations. In sum, the pretext of exposing the oppressed group to "civilization" is rendered absurd; the pretext of exposing the oppressed group to "the Protestant ethic and the spirit of capitalism"[1] is a clever ruse; and the idea that salvation is possible through total submission to oppression makes a mockery of Christian theology. Yet this is what Black people have been asked to accept about their American standing from white political leaders. More importantly, it's what Black people have been asked to accept about their religious standing

---

1. See Max Weber's classic on the Protestant notion that hard work in producing a more morally responsible society inevitably rewards both the individual and the nation regarding salvation, *The Protestant Ethic and the Spirit of Capitalism* (New York: Charles Scribner's Sons, 1958).

from white Christian leaders. Since what is fundamentally American has been so carefully wrapped in a thin veneer of Christian affirmation, one is not able to divorce American law from divine law. In other words, one is not able to divorce American racism from Christian theology. White men have taken Black people into the abyss of white supremacy. However, the path of righteousness directs Black people out of that abyss. It takes America and the world to the mountaintop of freedom. The God of Jesus Christ is not an oppressor but a liberator. Anything to the contrary is blasphemous, at best, and antibiblical, at worst.

In Job's recognition of the God who "does not oppress," he also identifies God's attribute of "justice and abundant righteousness." For not only is God just, but God is also righteous in that God does not approve of oppressive relationships but is revealed as the liberator, the deliverer of justice; and because of these attributes God is possessed of "abundant righteousness." This is because God consistently identifies with the captives, struggling with them to hew justice out of the stone of white avarice. In other words, the God of Black liberation chooses liberation over oppression. The God of Black liberation has chosen the oppression of Black people and made it God's own condition, seeking to chart a new course for humanity, and in so doing God's righteousness is revealed.

Not lost on the Black community is that God has chosen Black people in contemporary history as God chose the Israelites for liberation in biblical history. For the Black prophetic radical tradition, the tradition that agitates for social justice, this affirms that God's righteousness is not spiritual or otherworldly. As Mays notes,

> [Their] ideas are not otherworldly. They place one under obligation to adjust himself to a life of peace where all may enjoy the fruits necessary for resplendent living. They go far beyond the limits of race, but the needs of the race are met in the universality of the ideas of God presented.[2]

---

2. Benjamin E. Mays, *The Negro's God as Reflected in His Literature* (Westport, CT: Greenwood Publishing, 1969; orig., 1938), 82.

Here, God's universalism is not a hollow love extended to all humans but a *universalism-within-oppression* that extends God's liberating presence to every oppressed condition—including this one. This is why the God of biblical revelation is also the God of Black liberation! God's righteousness is affirmed in history as a liberator. And at the same time, universalism is rescued from descending into ideology. In other words, the white Christian community has characterized the Black–white relationship not as oppressive but as God's righteousness. *We are now free to think liberating thoughts without concern for being unrighteous.* The God of Black liberation puts us on the path of righteousness, knowing that our aspirations for liberation are neither alien nor sinful thoughts but are the essence of God's nature. The God of Black liberation does not root righteousness in a universal love of all humans but rather puts the world on notice that, instead of being second-class citizens of America, Black people are first-class children of God.

> They (whites) have always tried to kill us out. . . . If we had not been a chosen race of the Almighty God, we would have been gone long ago. Out on X Avenue where Negroes live, they won't put in sewers and give them the same protection as in white neighborhoods that are farther out. They call out race riots and shoot us, yet they expect us to be as good as they are. It makes me angry; on the other hand, it makes me have confidence in God. God is on our side.[3]

The confidence of Blacks in the power of God to liberate a nation from white privilege has never waned. Far from being an opiate, the emphasis here on Black people's chosen status is not a confidence in a heaven after physical death. Rather, God's righteousness is plunged into the plight of oppressed Blacks to demonstrate to the world that divine righteousness cannot be divorced from the socio-political liberation of Black people. Though Job puts God cosmically in the north, God does not stay there with regard to God's care for the social transformation of Black people. The field

---

3. Mays, *The Negro's God*, 82–84.

of dreams for God is in the "south," to take Black people to the "north," merging biblical revelation with Black liberation until there is no differentiation!

God's righteousness resides in God's prerogative to liberate oppressed humanity so that divine righteousness and the freedom of Black people are inseparable. It is that righteousness that is the pinnacle of divine activity in history. It is the cosmic and historic "yes" to human freedom. On July 2, 1827, the African Methodist Episcopal bishop Nathaniel Paul, torn and beset by the question of God's seeming indifference to the plight of Black people, answers his own question in his famous speech at The Abolition Rally in New York.

> Hark, while He answers from on high; hear Him proclaiming from the skies. "Be still and know that I am God! Clouds and darkness are around me; yet, righteousness and judgment are the habitation of my throne. I do my will and pleasure in the heavens above, and in the earth beneath; it is my sovereign prerogative to bring good out of evil and cause the wrath of man to praise me, and the remainder of that wrath I will restrain."[4]

Righteousness and judgment are the essence of divine reality. But more importantly, the divine will is executed "in the heavens above, *and* in the earth beneath," leaving no theological space to make the kingdom of heaven purely otherworldly. Rather, Nathaniel Paul is summoning the God of Black liberation to the earth via God's own articulation of divine righteousness that the will of God be executed below as well as above. This is why God beseeches us to strive for the kingdom of heaven first, and then righteousness. The socio-political imperative inherent in God's earthly activity affirms righteousness and devours ideology. This is why the wrath of God is restrained such that white folks will not be destroyed for their treatment of Black people insofar as God chooses "to bring good out of evil." By choosing good over evil before divine chastisement,

---

4. See Major J. Jones, *The Color of God: The Concept of God in Afro-American Thought* (Macon, GA: Mercer University Press, 1987), 34.

God makes the sovereign decision for Black liberation before white chastisement and in so doing makes known the primacy of the movement from Black bondage to Black freedom.

By bringing the good of Black liberation out of the evil of white supremacy, God's will is realized "on earth as it is in heaven." The new kingdom comes from the "north" and supplants the old earthly way of life—the white way of life. God's covenant with humanity means that a new structure for viewing human existence has been inaugurated. The difficulty in changing is not an excuse for forging a relationship with God without making the painstaking but necessary steps to shed human oppression for human liberation—a change God expects of us even in our universally fallen state. In this vein, Joseph Washington challenges white Christian ethicists:

> If Christian ethicists are to guide they will need to be engaged in direct change, beyond direct action. Though this be a "fallen world," it does not follow that the white models which serve to discern and defend what has been need be perpetuated.[5]

God's eternal law, the law of human freedom, demands a just theology to be its handmaiden. As such, white pontifications about heaven and Black docility are alien to divine righteousness. Christian theology does not justify an earthly tyrannical rule nor is it a flight to social irrelevancy. Rather, divine righteousness realizes itself in the social existence of Black humanity.

Divine Righteousness in a Racist Society

Divine righteousness in a racist society condemns racism as the highest sin. In this sense, the path of righteousness necessarily entails a radical uprooting of sin in Christian tradition. According to Bishop Berkeley's directive, sin is measured in a human's interior life and not in the social activity of human oppression. This

---

5. Joseph R. Washington, *The Politics of God* (Boston: Beacon Press, 1967), 148.

served the dual purpose of keeping Christian faith committed to the white way of life and gave Black people no theological basis for articulating their standing before God. Furthermore, it implied that God has no interest in the condition of Black people except to impress upon them the positive aspect of their condition. This was the theological choice of white Christian leadership to keep Black people "humble" and "meek"—the ideal attributes for true Christians! In short, sin has not been equated with racism but rather with trying to overthrow a racist rule! It has been distorted to serve the interests of white privilege, thereby sentencing sin to ideology.

Racism, however, has been America's biggest sin. The inability to see Black oppression not as salvific but evil has been white America's largest transgression. Its inability to recognize this egregious theological error is the reason why the "greatest" country in modern history still has a problem securing a lasting peace. As W. E. B. Du Bois noted at the turn of the twentieth century,

> The Nation has not yet found peace from its sins; the freedman has not yet found in freedom his promised land. Whatever good may have come in these years of change, the shadow of a deep disappointment rests upon the Negro people—a disappointment all the more bitter because the unattained ideal was unbounded save by the simple ignorance of a lowly people.[6]

The reason why the "Negro" has not yet found freedom in "his" promised land is because the land of the free and the home of the brave were never promised to him. The only promise that Black people were extended was tyrannical rule until the end of the world. Their righteousness was to find celestial fortune in being in close proximity to superior whites and to see the boundless dependence on white benevolence as a gift from God. With this perspective, America will never find peace from its sins. Divine righteousness will hold white America accountable for both its decadent inter-

---

6. W. E. B. Du Bois, *The Souls of Black Folks* (New York: Modern Library, 2003), 8.

action with Black people and its use of God to legitimate that interaction.

The God of Black liberation always strikes the decisive blow, instilling in Black people a righteous discontent with their condition. White America has failed to recognize that no tyrannical rule can keep those oppressed at peace with their situation. In other words, white America, in its superior wisdom, fails to see that no lasting peace can ever come to a country in which a segment of the society is forced to accept a second-class existence. This becomes particularly problematic for a country that touts its democratic ideals and constitutional freedoms. If democracy is rooted in liberty and truth, then no country can make that claim as its raison d'être while sustaining the myth of white superiority. Furthermore, no country can establish, let alone maintain, a society truly rooted in peace and yet hold other humans in bondage and deprive them of their constitutional rights and not incur the chastisement of a righteous God. Or worse, no country can live in true peace when it is founded on racism and remains in denial of the impact of such racism.

Deep-seated prejudices and the gruesome acts of violence by civilians and law enforcement officers continue to be the order of the day. The absence of peace continues while racial injustice exists in American life. As long as freedom eludes Black people, this country will never be at peace. In 1965, during a speech at a rally in Montgomery, Alabama, Martin Luther King Jr. alluded to this inability of American peace to manifest itself in a country still committed to white privilege a century on from the Emancipation Proclamation. We must strive for a society that is at peace with itself, a society that can live with its conscience, and "that will be the day not of the white man, not of the black man, that will be the day of man as man."[7] The unwillingness of white America to see the difference between racial tyranny and true peace is no longer contradictory; it is downright sinful!

---

7. Martin Luther King Jr., "Address to Montgomery Rally Participants at Alabama State Capital," March 25, 1965.

The cry for a racially just America has drawn a line in the battleground of freedom from which there is no retreat and no compromise. Whether it be on America's streets, its courtrooms, its educational institutions, or its religious institutions, the rallying cry today from the Black community that we will either be free or dead is a perfectly reasonable response to centuries of white hypocrisy.

What white America fails to recognize is that the source of Black rebellion is not Black people. What white Christian leadership fails to see is that "the spiritual strivings" of Black people entail more than highly charged prayers and the path of least resistance. Endemic to God's righteousness is the incessant restlessness instilled in Black people to secure their freedom. Divine righteousness reveals to the world God's plan for a liberated Black humanity and at the same time does not allow white America to live at "peace" with its racist rule. God's righteousness is revealed in the liberation struggle not only as divine preference but also as an opportunity to show America a moral picture of itself. It is an opportunity for God to use Black people to reveal God's glory and to bring down moral condemnation on a country for its continued sinfulness. Therein lies the spiritual dimension of the Black movement for freedom. As Du Bois notes,

> Merely a concrete test of the underlying principles of the great republic is the Negro Problem and the spiritual striving of the freedmen's sons is the travail of souls where burden is almost beyond the measure of their strength, but who bear it in the name of an historic race, in the name of this the land of their fathers' fathers, and in the name of human opportunity.[8]

Through Black people, God is showing America that no one can be righteous and racist at the same time. God is giving voice to the voiceless, and that voice is relentlessly hammering away at racial caste. White control has informed every major decision of national life, and especially the lives of Black people. It is the drive to normalize complete control over another race that is the highest sin.

---

8. Du Bois, *The Souls of Black Folks*, 14.

In response, whites have been attempting in each generation since slavery to maintain their "break" with racial bigotry, seeking conveniently to shift that bigotry to their forebears. This has been especially the preferred way of being in a post–civil rights era. But whites have also maintained those old structures of racial caste, especially in the realms of education and religion, where some school districts remain segregated and private schools in ritzy suburbs with a smattering of Blacks remain an option, and churches remain segregated. In religion as in politics, rational whites have taken false comfort and false hope in the civil rights movement as if it were being faithful to genuine religion and democracy, overlooking the truth that only insofar as the freedom of humanity is attuned to the freedom of God can there be discerned "righteousness and strength."[9]

The God of Black liberation brings righteousness and strength to Black people where weak white platitudes and half-hearted gestures are seen for their hypocrisy. It is what the slaves called "left-handed fellowship"—the opposite of the traditional right hand of fellowship that is extended when one becomes a candidate for baptism in the church. It is the recognition that God has shown Black people the sinful ways of whites and are gearing them up for the battle for freedom in a "free" country. Divine righteousness deadens Black people to white racist theories about the economic divide rooted in Black people's lack of industry, the political divide attributed to Black people's lack of political acumen, the intellectual divide attributed to Black people's intellectual inferiority, and the religious divide attributed to Jesus's whiteness! Black people know that white "success" has come off the backs of unpaid Black labor and exploitation. Divine righteousness reveals to the world that white privilege is antithetical to Christian faith and cannot live forever!

The Radical Demand of God's Love for the Oppressed

The radical demand of God's love for all life forms is evident in God's actions. It is radical, not in the summary denunciation by

---

9. Washington, *The Politics of God*, 165.

whites of Black protest that agitates for justice but a deviation from the norm that has been established by the human family. It is that radical love for humanity that God demonstrates aptly by becoming human in Jesus to atone for the sins of humanity. In biblical revelation, it is the ultimate sacrifice by God to prevent human perishing and to make eternal life possible (see John 3:16).

Having established racism as the highest sin, namely, in its brutal imposition physically and psychologically and in its use of the name of God as a pretext for Black oppression, God's love extends primarily to Blacks who are the victims of that racism, not whites, who continue to perpetuate the racism. When a bully on a playground imposes his will on a fellow student for no substantive reason, there is usually another student who intervenes on the side of the victimized student and stands up to the bully and saves that student from further bullying. In much the same way, when whites decided to impose their racist will on Blacks, God's love moves in support of Blacks. That love is demonstrated when God intervenes in history on the side of Blacks for their liberation. This is the meaning of God's righteousness in an oppressed context. This is how the manifestation of God's radical love manifests. This is why Carter G. Woodson proclaimed:

> The old worn-out theories as to man's relation to God and his fellowman, the system of thought which has permitted one man to exploit, oppress, and exterminate another and still be regarded as righteous must be discarded for the new thought of men as brethren and the idea of God as the lover of all mankind.[10]

Though not a theologian by trade, Woodson sees the hypocrisy in the universal treatment of God by white theologians who insist that God's love extends to all humans and that we all fall under the canopy of universal sin, making racism simply one sin among others. But for the God of Black liberation, racism is not simply

---

10. Carter G. Woodson, *The Mis-Education of the Negro* (Washington, DC: Associated Publishers, 1928), 149–50.

one sin among others. Such pronouncements are the product of a guilty white conscience, not the product of a liberating God who speaks into human history turning Black suffering into triumph, and makes known that Black people need not tarry over whether God is on their side. Partiality is a divine prerogative, divine justice! Thus, to treat the race problem as one that belongs side by side with all other sins is seen for what it is—an unashamed attempt to deflect attention away from the Black–white encounter. Joseph Washington notes,

> Loyalty to this order, not the order of creation or to the Kingdom of God, binds Christian ethicists. The doctrine of man as inescapably involved in sin becomes associated with the need for order and confused with the support of the current order. . . . The conclusion is that all men are involved in sin, the Negro is a man and so is involved in sin, and since sin is sin and not to be graded, the suffering of the Negro is just another instance of sin.[11]

For Washington, the white ethical community is more concerned with allegiance to the God of white privilege than with allegiance to the God of Black liberation. However, if whites were more interested in true human equality, they would not be trying to maintain white privilege but trying to bring about a more egalitarian society. By maintaining a lateral view of sin, whites not only diminish their activity in preventing human liberation but feign ignorance about their privilege. This is the biggest obstacle in realizing the kingdom. However, because God reveals Godself as a liberator, a Christian theology that equates the kingdom with Black suffering calls God to a day of reckoning. This is the meaning of God's demand for a radical love. By shunning objectivity in favor of subjectively standing with Blacks in the fight for self-determination, God undermines white privilege and seeks its demise. In this partial and unequivocal stand, the love demonstrated by God cannot be anything else but radical.

Despite the orthodoxy of universal sin, Black people encoun-

---

11. Washington, *The Politics of God*, 134.

tered a God who intervenes in history to change contexts of human domination, which means that God's love is clearly partial to the oppressed group. In so doing, God is also making the statement that racism is the highest priority. This is why Black people have no need for a God who loves all people. That love means accepting the liberating hand that God extends to all oppressed peoples as God did with the Israelites in Egyptian bondage. Moreover, the prophets displayed their unashamed commitment to justice and righteousness for the despised and abused. In that sense, Black people do not have any need for a God who has not identified totally with their blackness as the symbol of what it means to be human chattel and at the same time what it means to be a creation of God. As Dwight Hopkins notes,

> A just God brought righteousness in situations of conflict between the weak and the strong. For human property, righteousness corrected unjust relations and placed the Divinity squarely and unapologetically on the side of the oppressed. How could it be otherwise? Surely, since Yahweh heard their anguished cries and saw their cruel plight, Yahweh would "make things right." By bearing the innocent victims' burden, God stood with them and, furthermore, burst asunder systemic tentacles that literally choked the very lives of African American bondsmen and bondswomen.[12]

In standing with Black people as they take on the formidable evil of white supremacy, God's righteousness is demonstrated in God's sacrifice for "bearing the innocent victims' burden."

If nothing else, God's love is not universal; neither is it passive or static. Rather, God's love is active and extends beyond biblical history to contemporary history. Biblical revelation is an irrefutable expression of God's active love for the freedom of humanity and, conversely, God's disdain for systemic oppression. Whatever

---

12. Dwight N. Hopkins and George C. L. Cummings, *Cut Loose Your Stammering Tongue: Black Theology in the Slave Narratives* (Maryknoll, NY: Orbis Books, 1991), 16.

else may be said about God's righteousness must include the radical love that is endemic to that righteousness—a righteousness possessed of the two sharp edges of redemption and retribution. God's love redeems the oppressed by siding with them in their struggle for freedom. God's love becomes retributive when God refashions the kingdom out of white privilege and into human equality. This becomes especially significant when Christian theology has portrayed God and Jesus as siding with the bully over the victim. Such a theological perspective is nothing short of demonic.

> Black chattel underwent sadistic and savage treatment at the hands of fiendish white folk. Whites often gave slaves fifty to five hundred lashes and then poured salt, turpentine, or ground bricks into the fresh wounds. White males entered slave cabins and raped black women in the presence of their husbands. White males consistently "broke in" young black girls just arrived into puberty. Quite often slaves had their thumbs cut off for attempting to learn reading and writing. Slave traders purchased black women, snatched their children from their nursing breasts, and threw the babies on the side of the road to die.[13]

But let's not be fooled. Racist behavior in the name of God did not end with slavery. It has been evident even in a postslavery context that seemingly has no desire to relent. Unfortunately, George Floyd, who was "lynched" by a Minneapolis police officer, represents a long list of Black men who have not been protected but killed by white law enforcement. The scandal of this dastardly behavior toward Black people got not its highest condemnation but its highest approval from the white church. White theologians gave white demonism toward Black people either its most celebrated approval or did not make it a dimension of theological reflection at all. In either case, the God of Black liberation has sharpened the edge of the retribution blade, cutting through the

---

13. Hopkins and Cummings, eds., *Cut Loose Your Stammering Tongue*, 16.

falsehoods of white privilege and exposing it to the world. With the help of Black people, the God of Black liberation seeks retribution on a country for its hypocrisy in touting constitutional freedoms for all American citizens but treating Black people so savagely. Abolitionist David Walker takes a facetious swipe at the white Christian treatment of Blacks, saying that they should be appreciative for their treatment at the hands of white people.

> The Americans say, that we are ungrateful—but I ask them for heaven's sake, what should we be grateful to them for—for murdering our fathers and mothers? They certainly think we are a gang of fools. Those among them, who have volunteered their services for our redemption, though we are unable to compensate them for their labours, we nevertheless thank them from the bottom of our hearts, and we have our eyes steadfastly fixed upon them, and their labours of love for God and man.[14]

Walker is addressing the white theological understanding of redemption that holds that whites are doing God's work by civilizing a "gang of fools." But God's radical demand of love comes not through the approval of white vilification of Black people nor in a systemically racist national life, but in bringing about a new way of being human—an original way of being human—of returning humans to the original state of freedom that God intended. Thus, to speak of God's righteousness is to speak of God's love for oppressed humanity as anchored in ending Black people's demonized status. Anything other than that is the platitude-oriented universal love of white theology that is not part of God's redemptive plan. Tolstoy puts universal love in more practical terms.

> We are all brothers, but I live on a salary paid me for prosecuting, judging, and condemning the thief or the prostitute whose existence the whole tenor of my life tends to bring about, and who I know ought not to be punished but reformed. We are all

---

14. David Walker, *The Appeal to the Coloured Citizens of the World* (Baltimore, MD: Black Classic Press, 1993; orig., 1830), 75.

> brothers, but I live on a salary I gain by collecting taxes for the needy laborers to be spent on the luxuries of the rich and idle. We are all brothers, but I take a stipend for preaching a false Christian religion, which I do not myself believe in, and which only serves to hinder men from understanding true Christianity. I take a stipend as priest or bishop for deceiving men in the matter of the greatest importance to them.[15]

Thus, Black people have heard with painful familiarity white platitudes about loving your neighbor as yourself; but, as Tolstoy outlines, when it comes to sharing the resources of the earth, the distribution is decidedly one-sided. No human being with even a novice social conscience can see such hypocrisy as love. More importantly, not only do Black people hear these acerbic appeals to unity and peace, but God hears them as well. Furthermore, God sees the diametric opposite of that love carried out by white leadership, and the radical demand of God's love urges liberating activity to right the wrong created by white racism. As Cone notes,

> Blacks cannot adhere to a view of God that will weaken their drive for liberation. This means that in a racist society, we must insist that God's love and God's righteousness are two ways of talking about the same reality. Righteousness means that God is addressing the black condition; love means that God is doing so in the interests of both blacks and whites. The blackness of God points to the righteousness of God, as well to the love of God.[16]

Therefore, God's radical love demands that Black people fight the good fight for freedom (redemption) and demands that whites become "Black" by opting for Black freedom, not white privilege, or risk becoming "hardened-heart" pharaohs and watching their army drown in the Red Sea (retribution).

---

15. Leo Tolstoy, *The Kingdom of God Is within You* (Lincoln, NE: University of Nebraska Press, 1984), 119.

16. James H. Cone, *A Black Theology of Liberation* (New York: Orbis Books, 1990), 72–73.

The Righteousness of God as the Wrath of God

In a racist nation, God's righteousness cannot be separated from God's wrath. The two are not in dialectical relationship, nor do they go together. They are actually one. It was not an error for the white theological community to treat God's righteousness in conjunction with God's wrath. Yet, the treatment itself from the plantation to today has been directed at Black people that God's wrath would visit them for seeking to subvert their condition, and at whites that God's wrath would visit them if they do not maintain racial caste—thus making righteousness and wrath synonymous. In no way has God's righteousness been more the meaning of God's wrath than through an American political system that creates racist laws. In this sense, the white political community has been just as complicit as the white theological community. By legalizing slavery, segregation, and now the all-too-familiar "rule of law," America's societal laws have been the political extension of the laws of God. The ultimate intent has been to perpetuate white privilege and have Black people punished by the criminal justice system and kept in line with the God of white supremacy's wrath for simply wanting to be free. The political system has also been a shrewd way to diminish Black fervor for freedom—a form a chicanery not lost on Frederick Douglass.

> Slaveholders have made it almost impossible for the slave "to commit any crime, known either to the laws of God or to the laws of man." If he steals he takes his own; if he kills the master, he imitates only the heroes of the revolution. Slaveholders I hold to be individually and collectively responsible for all the evils which grow out of the horrid relation, and I believe they will be so held at the judgment, in the sight of a just God. Make a man a slave and you rob him of moral responsibility.[17]

---

17. Frederick Douglass, *My Bondage and My Freedom* (New York: Miller, Orton, and Mulligan, 1855), 191. See also Mays, *The Negro's God*, 124.

Douglass discerns the visceral effect as to how a theology of divine wrath for Black rebellion limits responsibility in Blacks to wage a full-fledged struggle for liberation. He was also able to connect that lack of social responsibility with American laws that are inherently racist. More significantly, one is able to see the impact that white Christian leadership has had on the theological psyche of Black people. There was a sense in which Black people came to understand the wrath of God in terms of their rebellion against an institution that they found immoral. This is largely why the tenor of Black worship has been so otherworldly: it was not just the expectant hope for a life that was far better than the hell they lived on earth; it was also a way to commune with God and to spare the possible wrath that came from wanting to be free in a nation whose God said they should be slaves eternally. This is another example of a *negative goodness* referenced by Mays.

> These ideas [of God] . . . fall in the category of the compensatory because they tend to produce a negative goodness based wholly on a fear of the wrath of God in the next world. They make it easier for the adherent to escape social responsibility here, and they probably had this effect on many during the heated years between 1830 and 1850.[18]

The God of Black liberation has a different wrath in mind. The scandal of the wrath of God has not been Black people's lack of social responsibility but white Christian leadership making them feel guilty for embracing that responsibility. The scandal has not been Black people "taking" when they had been deprived of basic human rights but white Christian leadership's connecting that "taking" to sin. The scandal has not been Black people striving for freedom but white Christian leadership making that striving a means of "confirming" Black people's corrupted morality. In short, the righteousness of God in a racist society that is itself morally corrupt holds the height of divine contempt not for Black people but for white people!

---

18. Mays, *The Negro's God*, 124.

When God gives us the opportunity to govern, that opportunity should enhance life rather than limit it. Given that white supremacy is based on constructing laws that legitimate white dominance, it is found wanting in the eyes of God and unleashes God's wrath. In fact, the real tragedy of white supremacy has been its insistence on the utter deprivation of humanity in Black people under the banner of Christendom and God. This is why it has been the focus of the God of Black liberation. God reveals that racial caste is not God's will insofar as God reveals that a humanity created in freedom nullifies racial caste as a normative way of being human. It is the captive who occupies God's attention, not the despot. It is the despised who occupy God's attention, not the tyrant. Through Jesus's suffering at the hands of those content with a stifling status quo, God makes clear that the oppressed are not alone in their quest for human dignity. Cone reminds us,

> Both Jesus and blacks were publicly humiliated, subjected to the utmost indignity and cruelty. They were stripped, in order to be *deprived of dignity*, then paraded, mocked and whipped, pierced, derided and spat upon, tortured for hours in the presence of jeering crowds for popular entertainment. In both cases, the purpose was to strike terror in the subject community.[19]

Indeed, the wrath of God is incensed at the deprivation of dignity that has come to characterize Black suffering, but, more to the point, God is incensed at depriving Black people of dignity in the name of God. In other words, to speak of God's righteousness is to give humans the freedom to construct a nation, but it is also to speak of God's wrath when that construction becomes oppressive. The wrath of God is exacted on tyrannical rulers and not on those whom the tyrants deprive of dignity.

It is interesting that neither the wrath of God on Blacks for their previous treatment of whites nor on Blacks for using Chris-

---

19. James Cone, *The Cross and the Lynching Tree* (Maryknoll, NY: Orbis Books, 2011), 31.

tian faith to enslave another race of people before being enslaved by whites has ever been used by "erudite" white theologians in their treatises on the rationale of African abduction. In this sense, Black people are innocent in history and in the eyes of God for the treatment they have received in "the land of the free and the home of the brave." America has not been about Black redemption but white oppression. Cone continues,

> As Jesus was an innocent victim of mob hysteria and Roman imperial violence, many African Americans were innocent victims of white mobs, thirsting for blood in the name of God and in defense of segregation, white supremacy, and the purity of the Anglo-Saxon race. Both the cross and the lynching tree were symbols of terror, instruments of torture and execution, reserved primarily for slaves, criminals and insurrectionists—the lowest of the low in society.[20]

And yet whites would have Blacks think that the God of Jesus Christ would desire Blacks to fully capitulate to this existence of torture, execution, or just outright submission to white rule as an extension of God's will. Rather than putting forward a substantive treatment of the righteousness of God, the white Christian establishment has put forward a racist treatment of God's righteousness that does not represent the God of biblical revelation.

Not only was the deprivation of dignity seen in lynching Black people, for instance, sending the message that they should stay in their place, but it also depicted Black people as innate criminals. Yet how is Black "criminality" to be measured in a racist society? When slaves ran away from the plantation, it was considered illegal in the eyes of white politicians, but was it illegal in God's eyes? If the God of Jesus Christ came to side with the oppressed and suffer the cruel indignities for seeking to uproot the current order and to bring about a more liberated existence for the lowly and despised, then the Black restlessness with bondage not only affirmed the God of biblical revelation but affirmed their being created in freedom.

---

20. Cone, *The Cross and the Lynching Tree*, 31.

Thus, given the daily indignities of injustice, Black people had to either "steal" to be free or procure the basic necessities denied them on a daily basis on the plantation—and American life. As Hopkins describes.

> The slaves, "didn't get nothing but fat meat and corn bread and molasses. And they got tired of that same old thing." Consequently, they had to "illegally" enter the hen house to get chickens or the smokehouse to get hams or the vegetable patches to procure adequate nourishment. In a word, they had to define and develop a culture of resistance, a way of life to survive slavery's onslaught on their humanity. As one former slave asks: "That ain't stealing, is it?"[21]

In the defense of this slave, another slave puts it in more succinct terms:

> All you hear now is "bout de nigger stealin" from dese here po' white devils. De whole cause of stealin' an' crime is 'caused dey fo'ced the nigger to do hit in dem back days. . . . White folks certainly taught niggers to steal. If they had given them enough to eat dey wouldn' have no cause to steal.[22]

And in the ultimate rebuttal to the "stealing" ethic of white theologians, ex-slave Josephine Howard places stealing in its larger context regarding the real sinners.

> Dey allus done tell us it am wrong to lie and steal, but why did de white folks steal my mammy and her mammy? Dey lives clost to some water, somewhere over in Africy. . . . Dat de sinfulles' stealin' dey is.[23]

---

21. Hopkins and Cummings, eds., *Cut Loose Your Stammering Tongue*, 37–38.
22. Hopkins and Cummings, eds., *Cut Loose Your Stammering Tongue*, 38.
23. Hopkins and Cummings, eds., *Cut Loose Your Stammering Tongue*, 38.

Howard, clearly the victim of having a formal education "stolen" from her, is rightly able to discern that the "stealing" in which Black people admittedly engage should be viewed in the larger context in which their rights are nonexistent. I ask, then, is it "stealing" or is it what the slaves termed "taking"? In sum, that has been the Black theological antidote for Christian racism—to present a mirror that shows whites their much larger sins in the eyes of a just God!

Finally, divine wrath emanates from God's love to fallen humanity but more particularly to oppressed humanity. God's wrath does not mean being sent to the dungeons of hell for not genuflecting before white people. God's wrath comes in the dawn of a new age where "the last shall be first." It is the day of vindication, not for whites who are trying to bring "heathen" Blacks, who remain stubbornly resistant to being "civilized," into the Christian fold. It is the day of vindication for Black people in which the "weeping and gnashing of teeth" will be for racists who persist in putting forward a society of white privilege. While the Gospel proclaims "release to the captives and . . . to let the oppressed go free" (Luke 4:18–19) its parallel in the Old Testament as read by Jesus at the synagogue to his people announces "the year of the LORD's favor, and the day of vengeance of our God" (Isa 61:1–2). In other words, God's penultimate concern is to proclaim "a year of favor" or that divine wrath is on the horizon. But God's ultimate concern is based on a "day" or the immediacy of vindication for those held in bondage who are "heavy laden," for those enduring the daily indignities of oppressed existence that the day of vindication is imminent.[24]

That God will avenge the horrors of their existence and bring "liberty to the captives," as we read in Exodus, and continuing through to the prophets, including Isaiah, through Jesus to Paul and, more importantly, to Black life today—Black people in America, who have had to and continue to labor under the prom-

---

24. Gustavo Gutiérrez, *The God of Life* (Maryknoll, NY: Orbis Books, 1991), 7.

ise of freedom since the Emancipation Proclamation, but who are yet to receive "the promises of democracy."

The reneging on those promises by the U.S. government is still mainly ignored by America's religious institutions when they continue to remain in collusion with racist demagogues. From their perspective, God either condones their bigoted ways or God's wrath could never be meant for such a "successful" people. Certainly a God who is the essence of freedom would not sanction a racist society, nor would a God who is the essence of freedom sanction a society of human domination. To speak of God as a condoner of Black oppression is to speak of an idolatrous white god who is as sincere about a liberated Black humanity as most white Americans. That should come as no surprise. American, and even global society, is built on the myth of white superiority. But because that God has been presented to Black people and the world as the God of Jesus Christ, American society has earned the day of vindication from God. In light of this perspective, Cone asks,

> Is it possible to understand what God's love means for the oppressed without making *wrath* an essential ingredient of that love? What could love possibly mean in a racist society except the righteous condemnation of everything racist?[25]

Thus, for the God of Black liberation divine righteousness can only be a "vindication" of every attempt on the part of Black people to liberate themselves and to aid in the destruction of everything racist in society. The wrath of God brings the good news that white deprivation of dignity no longer holds sway over Black bodies.

---

25. Cone, *Black Theology of Liberation*, 69

5

The Path of Justice

The path of justice has been a particularly arduous journey. The journey has been made more formidable in a nation that is considered theoretically a paragon of freedom, but practically it is a paragon of acute hypocrisy, because Black people were never brought to America to be free citizens. In fact, Black people were not brought to America to be citizens at all; they were bought to America to be free laborers and were never to share in the economic gains of colonial life. Theologically, they were to be unpaid laborers until the end of the world. Thus, in the vision that European men had for the building of a nation, first as an extension of English nobility and following the American Revolution as a society of free market reforms, Black people were never meant to advance in fruitful nationhood with their white brothers and sisters.

All racial laws in American society, beginning with the slave codes, were created not to make a society free of race but to make a sharp distinction between white and Black humanity. In fact, Black people were chattel and not considered human beings at all. In other words, the only humanity in colonial life was white people. Thus, while there have been two humanities from the inception of American society, there has been only one humanity in America practically—white humanity!

The dehumanization of Black people in the American democratic experiment legitimized that acute hypocrisy. How is it that a free market society could tout its desire to be free from English occupation and also hold Black people as slaves? Furthermore, how could a people who used Black people to help them win independence from Britain continue to hold those same Black people in bondage? How could a new nation founded on democracy continue to treat Black people as nonhumans? How could a new nation develop a pledge of allegiance to a flag that contained the words "liberty and justice for all," when, in reality, liberty and justice have been only for white people? America has not given liberty and justice to Black people, and any measures that have been obtained have come after long and protracted direct engagement with white political and religious leaders. Certainly this contradiction had to be addressed by the white American community, but their biggest mistake was not to admit the contradiction and treat Black people as human beings but, instead, commit themselves even more ardently to a "white" nation under God.

Nowhere has this been more the case than in white America's Christian institutions. By using Christian faith to legitimate white superiority, it enlisted God as the ultimate validator of the white way of life. In short, it committed the highest sin by making a just God, a God who comes to break the chains of oppression, into an unjust God who condones the reduction of Black people to chattel. To this end, to internalize this contradiction, so-called independent Black churches were formed not to create free Blacks but to create pious Blacks whose hopes for freedom could only be realized after physical death. In so doing, Christian faith severely compromised a well-informed liberation platform.

America has been an unjust country not only legally but also *theologically*. In other words, the path of justice, especially for a Christian nation, must deal decisively with the question of divine justice. For Blacks, this has meant a strategic act to take the white notion of justice and stand it on its head—to make justice a concrete reality for all Americans. Ironically, that charge has been led publicly by a few Black courageous ministers in each generation who gave themselves over to a "militant" faith and a struggle for justice that surely was not going to achieve its goals without tremendous physical and mental sacrifice.

In 1843, when Presbyterian minister Henry Highland Garnet

sounded the rallying cry for Black people with the words, "Let your motto be Resistance! Resistance! RESISTANCE!" it was a call for steadying Black people to the task of freeing themselves from white tyranny through one means only—confrontation! But he was also removing the veil of white proclamations of justice in an America that had staunchly committed itself to Black dehumanization. Despite that injustice, Garnet imbued in Blacks an even stronger commitment to freedom.

> Tell them in a language which they cannot misunderstand of the exceeding sinfulness of slavery and of a future judgment, and of the righteous retributions of an indignant God. Inform them that all you desire is FREEDOM, and nothing else will suffice. Do this, and forever after cease to toil for the heartless tyrants, who give you no other reward but stripes and abuse. If they then commence [the] work of death, they, and not you, will be responsible for the consequences. You had far better all die—*die immediately*—than live [as] slaves, and entail your wretchedness upon your posterity.[1]

Garnet was one of the forerunners of militant leadership standing American hypocrisy on its head with a decisive stand for freedom—even if it meant physical death! Garnet and other abolitionists such as Denmark Vesey, Toussaint L'Ouverture of Haiti, Nat Turner, Joseph Cinque, and Madison Washington were able to turn a repressive social condition into a win-win situation. Backed by the God of Black liberation, their lives became a living sacrifice similar to that of Jesus; and, furthermore, if assassinated in the process, they would no longer be shackled by the infernal chains of white enslavement. They would have earned the God of Black liberation's highest commendation for their labors. Garnet understood that the God of the Bible is not who white preachers said God was and, in light of that, knew that the God of biblical revelation

---

1. Taken from Gayraud S. Wilmore, *Black Religion and Black Radicalism: An Interpretation of the Religious History of African Americans* (Maryknoll, NY: Orbis Books, 1998), 120.

was a God of justice who had empowered the Black community to break the back of white supremacy. This is why Garnet knew it was his calling to inspire Blacks to the same end, even in the face of what would surely be white backlash. Garnet was committed unto death to expose the white American contradiction between its pronouncements and the application of those pronouncements. He knew that a "good nigger" to whites was a sinful nigger to God, and what was justice to white people was anathema to God. Therefore, the Black struggle for justice has always been rooted in exposing the contradiction between white proclamations and practice.

Garnet also saw God as a God of retributive justice, invoking chastisement on whites for their treatment of Blacks, which would become a major theological theme emanating from militant Black leadership. The righteous indignation that white preachers taught Blacks would visit them for resisting their bondage had been reversed. The God of Black liberation began to imbue Blacks with an incessant yearning for a return to their original state of freedom, and no amount of white theological teaching, no matter how erudite, would or could derail the train of Black freedom. In other words, the source of Black empowerment to realize a just America came from the same God whom whites maintained had willed Black bondage. Thus, the liberation of Black people and the liberation of God from racist manipulations are twin poles grounded in God's creative intent. The two are so interrelated that to speak of one is to speak of the other! The path of justice provides Blacks with an alternative—a justice movement that is engineered by the God of Black liberation that is as eternal as God's reign. Given its eternal ground and its omnipotent prowess, it will outduel and outlive white supremacy.

God's Presence in the Stand for Justice

In the spirit of "tell them in a language they cannot misunderstand," confronting white racism with a noncompromising posture has always been crucial to the Black quest for justice. It requires, as stated above, a win-win mentality in the wake of white backlash that has included not just a severe lashing or economic reprisal but the end of human life itself. Thousands of Black people and scores of Black leaders have exited this world via white mobs, assassins, or police officers as examples of what will happen to Black people who refuse to "stay in their place." No one understood this better than Martin Luther King Jr. He was a young man at the height of the Montgomery Bus Boycott. At the end of a late January evening in 1956, a month into the boycott, Dr. King received a threatening call from a white man who told him: "Leave Montgomery immediately if you have no wish to die." King sat at his kitchen table while his family slumbered and had a special session with God. He said to God, essentially, that he was in Montgomery taking a stand for what he thought was right. But he also stated that he was afraid and that if he showed fear publicly, then those who looked to him for leadership would begin to falter and the boycott would fail because of the white community's greatest weapon against Black protest—fear! He told God that he had nothing left to give and was at the end of his line. But at that moment, King got a response at his kitchen table. He called it experiencing "the presence of the Divine as I had never experienced it before." He heard a voice clearly and without mistaken identity say to him, "Martin Luther, stand up for righteousness. Stand up for justice. Stand up for truth. And lo, I will be with you, even until the end of the world." King said that from that point of the movement forward he had been prepared for whatever calamity came his and the movement's way. It was then that "My uncertainty disappeared and I was ready to face anything."[2]

The voice that King heard was indeed the voice of God. But it was not the God of segregation or white privilege. If it were, the movement would never have begun. It was the voice of the God of Black liberation assuring King that the cause of leading a despised people to freedom was God's cause as well. It was the God of biblical revelation who favored human dignity over human exploitation

---

2. Martin Luther King Jr., *Stride Toward Freedom: The Montgomery Story* (San Francisco: Harper & Row, 1986; orig., 1958).

and who favored Black liberation over white supremacy. Because that God voiced the hope of the oppressed, the God of biblical revelation has been for Black people the God of Black liberation. The God of Black liberation is the contemporary expression of the God of biblical revelation. For just as the God of biblical revelation was primarily concerned with reversing the condition of "the least of these" and was a champion of the oppressed, so too is the God of Black liberation in the contemporary scene in America.

The voice King heard told him specifically to stand up for justice and righteousness. For God's reign cannot enter into the world divorced from these two realities. Justice for the oppressed is the historical medium of human liberation while righteousness is the transhistorical medium of human liberation. Both intersect at the divine and human working in tandem to end societal injustice. Both justice and righteousness collaborate in the book of the reluctant prophet Amos, in which he said, "let justice roll down like waters, and righteousness like an ever-flowing stream" (Amos 5:24). This passage was a favorite quote of King, which he used in his famous "I Have a Dream" speech at the March on Washington. Amos's critique of world oppression was brutal. But more importantly, his critique of popular religion was just as piercing.

> *I hate, I despise your festivals,*
>   *and I take no delight in your solemn assemblies.*
> *Even though you offer me your burnt offerings and grain offerings,*
>   *I will not accept them;*
> *and the offerings of well-being of your fatted animals*
>   *I will not look upon.*
> *Take away from me the noise of your songs;*
>   *I will not listen to the melody of your harps.* (Amos 5:21–23)

Amos demonstrates his prophetic edge here more than in any other part of his book. He takes straight aim at the popular religion of Israel, who had forgotten that God had led them out of Egypt, and their expression of faith had become too ritualistic and emotionally exuberant. They put worship of God over societal injustice and artistic expression in song over the pursuit of freedom. The covenant God made with Abraham to be Israel's people was to see them out of Egypt and into the land God promised—and to be with them unconditionally until the end of the world. Israel's job was to let God lead them to that land of promise and to be obedient to God and not to the world. Yet Israel strayed from God's plan for their freedom and became seduced by the religious expression of the complacent. What made the call to justice and righteousness so profound was Amos's call for a new way of being a people, a new way of being in relationship with God (5:21–23). In other words, God was saying through Amos that you cannot serve two Gods—you must choose between justice and righteousness on the one hand or popular religiosity on the other hand.

King spoke of a similar lethargy regarding religious leadership in Montgomery at the start of the boycott. He lamented over "an appalling lack of unity" among Montgomery's leaders, the disintegration of the Citizens Coordinating Committee "due to a lack of tenacity on the part of the leaders" and "the indifference of the educated group," who undoubtedly did not want to get involved in the boycott for fear of damaging their relationship with the "good" whites in Montgomery. Educated Blacks, to be sure, saw themselves as the fruits of a previous struggle. They labored under the misconception that if other Blacks would simply follow their example, racial protest would not be necessary. For other educated Blacks, the fear of economic reprisal was a very real possibility if they publicly protested segregation. However, King mostly cited apathy as the primary reason for avoiding racial struggle. What many of the educated class failed to understand, like many today, is that formal education is not a panacea. It is a gateway to a better quality life materially, but it alone does not bring justice to a people who lag behind in every major arena of human existence due not to lack of industry but to a lack of opportunities.

But more to the point, for King, "the apparent apathy of the Negro ministers presented a special problem." At the core of this apathy was the notion that ministers should not get involved in movements of social change, let alone lead them. Their devotion to God was rooted in a "spiritual" relationship that touted a fiery presentation of the gospel and that God, in seeing sincere worship, would bring about justice. In this sense, Black Christianity had become less concerned with justice and more concerned with institutional success. It had become "neo-churchy" and less social in its outlook. Justice had been supplanted by "fire and brimstone," and righteousness had been supplanted by offerings and pageantry. For King, this approach to faith by Black Christian leadership lacked the vitality to bring about justice for Black people.

> A faithful few had always shown a deep concern for social problems, but too many had remained aloof from the area of social responsibility. Much of this indifference, it is true, stemmed from a sincere feeling that ministers were not supposed to get mixed up in such earthly, temporal matters as social and economic improvement; they were to "preach the gospel," and keep men's minds centered on "the heavenly."[3]

King, like most other prophetic leaders, understood that the path of justice had been booby-trapped by Christian theology. He understood that Christian faith had been geared toward comfort in a nation of acute injustice using heaven as its biggest selling point. Consequently, the most potent weapon for achieving justice—faith—had been robbed of its ability to be the quintessential force for justice. Surely, the Black ministers who understood their role to save souls were sincere in their faith. Such an understanding of faith had been in the making for several generations before King's era and continues to hinder Black strivings for justice today. Black ministers' opposition to social change is rooted in their internalization of the long-standing axiom of white Christianity that religion is asocial and ahistorical. What most Black ministers have not been able to see is that the intent of that axiom is to diminish Black people's power to overcome white racism. Thus, King understood—even when he struggled with his father's fire-and-brimstone approach in his childhood and adolescent years

---

3. King Jr., *Stride toward Freedom*, 35.

at Ebenezer Baptist Church in Atlanta—that one of the biggest opponents to the Black fight for justice was, ironically, Christian faith itself! King found such an approach a betrayal of biblical revelation's call for justice for the disinherited. Any religion that professes to be concerned with the souls of men and is not concerned with the slums that damn them, the economic conditions that strangle them, and the social conditions that cripple them is a dry-as-dust religion.[4]

Unfortunately, this sincere inclination on the part of ministers still haunts the church today. It still operates out of a celebratory, "highly favored," and asocial worldview. The theology of the church is still given over to a white-centered view of Christian faith, including enduring images of a white Jesus proudly adorning church walls. Fire and brimstone are still the crowd favorite over and against more prophetic and thought-provoking sermons. The church is still much more of a center for refuge and comfort than a center for social transformation. No matter the level of sincerity, one is able to detect a clear historical line from the theology of the white church in plantation life to today.

While I recognize the need for both refuge and comfort in a nation so overtly hostile to the achievement of Black aspiration, to make that dimension of ecclesiastical life the cornerstone of Christian practice sends a counterproductive and aborted message to parishioners. It is counterproductive in that it has created an unnecessary conflict between Black militant and Black pastoral leadership where the latter is unable to wrap its mind around a faith that frees Black people to agitate for social justice. It sends an aborted message to parishioners in that it does not open them up to freedom on earth as an essential aspect of the gospel. After several generations of this aborted expression of faith, parishioners began to think that this truncated version of the gospel is the totality of the gospel message. This is not only what King was faced with in Montgomery but what he was faced with throughout his career. While there were a few ministers who gravitated to the pro-

---

4. King, *Stride Toward Freedom*, 36.

phetic call for justice and were not afraid to publicly challenge the white power structure, the overwhelming majority of Black ministers refused to embrace it, given that their religious indoctrination prevented them from seeing the biblical mandate for justice. For those who did see that justice eluded Blacks, they still did not see the realization of justice as a function of religion or the church. In fact, all of our stalwart leaders had icy relationships with church leaders because of the former's primary allegiance to justice and righteousness as opposed to popular religiosity. In each of them, an Amos moment had occurred, and they could no longer hold their peace regarding justice for Black people. They understood the quest for justice as a ministerial calling, despite the way white Christian leadership had gutted the faith of its liberating essence and had influenced Black churches to unwittingly follow suit. They were convinced, and rightly so, that a "noise of solemn assemblies" religion, no matter how sincere, could not bring any measure of justice to Black people.

Now, the church must return to its prophetic roots and respond positively to Amos's call for justice and righteousness. It must be more committed to developing a language that prophetically condemns racism and announces the new kingdom rooted in justice and righteousness. Furthermore, this new liberating language must not be a weekday language; it must become a Sunday morning language that makes its way into the pulpit and into the liturgy of the church. This challenge is endemic to all religions, not just Christianity. All religions possess a conservative component that frowns on collective expressions of faith. Their leadership must understand that faith is concerned with more than saving souls and with emotional exuberance. All sermons should not end at the cross, but, perchance they do, it is to point us not just to the resurrection of the individual soul but to the sanctuaries, the streets, the courtrooms, and the boardrooms, as we seek the resurrection of a crucified people suffering under a tyrannical rule masquerading as a democracy.

One God... Two Histories

The [ultimate] symbol of justice is Justitia, the Roman goddess of justice. In most depictions, she is imaged with evenly balanced scales in her left hand, a sword in her right hand, and a blindfold over her eyes. The evenly balanced scales suggest that justice is a national gift of birthright to all citizens; the sword is to defend justice against those seeking to subvert it, and the blindfold is indicative of justice for all, regardless of physical appearance, race, gender, religion, or national origin. Although it touts that it is a country of justice, America has failed on all counts. American justice has been particularly contradictory when it comes to racial justice. In fact, Black people were not part of the framers' discussion,[5] nor were they considered in the conversation on justice. In short, Black people have experienced an American justice system that was never meant for them. More directly, the image of justice that best represents American history is one of a male—white, clean-shaven, arrogant, and racist—with no blindfold, highly unevenly balanced scales in his left hand, and a semi-automatic weapon in his right hand, ready to use on any Black person (or white) who dares challenge the hypocrisy of that image.

Consequently, there have been two lived histories under God. White political scientist Andrew Hacker brought this version of justice to the nation's conscience with his highly acclaimed work, *Two Nations: Black and White, Separate, Hostile, Unequal*.[6] The book sparked a range of emotions, particularly among those in the white community, who thought the book would only further the cause of leftists and rabble-rousers who were seeking publicity with this same argument. Hacker persuasively made the case

---

5. The framers are defined by the National Archives as those fifty-five individuals who were appointed to be delegates to the 1787 Constitutional Convention and took part in drafting the proposed Constitution of the United States. Of the fifty-five framers, only thirty-nine were signers of the Constitution.

6. Andrew Hacker, *Two Nations: Black and White, Separate, Hostile, Unequal* (New York: Ballantine Books, 1992).

that in every major category of social, economic, and political life, white people were far more privileged than Black people. Additionally, Hacker did not take the usual route of white scholars who maintained that these highly unequal indexes were the result of the diminished endowment of Black people. Rather, Hacker affirmed the equal endowment of Black people and postulated that these conditions have been created with malice aforethought and are systemically grounded in white racial entitlement. Hacker was pointed in his conclusion that "America is inherently a 'white' country: in character, in structure, in culture." The bulk of the work, however, was dedicated to pointing out the racial blindness of his white brothers and sisters.

> If white Americans regard the United States as their nation, they also see it beset with racial problems they feel are not of their making. Some contrast current conditions with earlier times, when blacks appeared more willing to accept a subordinate status. Most whites will protest that they bear neither responsibility nor blame for the conditions blacks face. Neither they nor their forebears ever owned slaves, nor can they see themselves as having held anyone back or down. Most white Americans believe that for at least the last generation blacks have been given more outright advantages. Moreover, few white Americans feel obliged to ponder how membership in the major race gives them powers and privileges.[7]

Hacker captured the thinking about the responsibility of most white Americans regarding their collusion in the racial denial of Blacks—none! He also captured their thinking regarding their racial privilege—none! They found greater comfort in conceding the inhumane treatment of Blacks to their slaveholding fathers but bear no responsibility in the contemporary divide between the races.

Not surprisingly, the white evangelical community, the largest white Christian body in the United States, followed suit. In their work *Divided by Faith: Evangelical Religion and the Problem of Race*

---

7. Hacker, *Two Nations*, 4.

in America,[8] Michael Emerson and Christian Smith conducted a study of the racial views of white evangelicals, which demonstrated how Christian faith has been the handmaiden of white racism. The majority of white evangelicals interviewed maintained that, although a racial problem does exist in America, the problem was not so much their or their church's bigotry and depiction of Black people, but rather government entitlement programs that distribute unearned benefits to Black people, like food stamps and welfare, and Black leaders who continue to fan the flames of racial discontent where none is present. They are convinced that the days of white privilege are gone and that human problems are largely personal. Unbeknownst to them, these personal problems stem from white Christian leadership in colonial life. White evangelicals not only interpret race issues using accountable freewill individualism and relationalism, but they often find structural explanations irrelevant or even wrongheaded.[9]

Both works demonstrate that whites have not only inherited a privileged existence but are in denial about it. More importantly, by virtue of the way white privilege is taught—that there is none—white people are often so blinded by their own racial ideology that they are unable to see how to get out of it or even the need to get out of it. In other words, whites, by virtue of the way they are socially and theologically taught about their community's existence, do not possess the ability to critically analyze their bigotry and, therefore, cannot be depended on to put forward any egalitarian view of justice.

America is in fact two histories in practice—one white and privileged; the other Black and oppressed.

A more poignant analysis demands that instead of two nations, America has been in reality only one nation—white! Men of color and women have had no legitimate stake in national life, not

---

8. Michael Emerson and Christian Smith, *Divided by Faith: Evangelical Religion and the Problem of Race in America* (New York: Oxford University Press, 2000).

9. Emerson and Smith, *Divided by Faith*, 78.

because they have not earned it or been visible but, in the words of Ralph Ellison, because others "refuse to see me." That invisibility has been the most prominent manifestation of injustice, as Blacks have been ostracized from the major institutions in American life. They are only included more visibly when tokenism is the aim, making that institution appear less racist. It has become customary since the end of slavery that the majority of Blacks have been employed as subordinates and civil servants—the jobs white people would not work! When it comes to a representative presence in the major political and economic institutions of national life, however, Blacks are conspicuously missing. David Walker puts it more succinctly:

> We, who have enriched their country with our blood and tears—have dug up gold and silver, for them and their children, from generation to generation, and are in more miseries than any other people under heaven, are not seen, but by comparatively, a handful of the American people.[10]

Walker is laying bare what many Blacks see as American justice in action—a willful, systemic attempt to use the machinations of power to maintain white privilege to the detriment of Black strivings for justice. Certainly, white men have been the major decision makers on vital policy that has essentially enforced white privilege and diminished Black opportunity. Black men have been stereotyped as unintelligent brutes, and Black women have been stereotyped as difficult, immoral, sexually promiscuous, and evil temptresses. As a result, a pitiable mentality emerged in the minds of most whites about Blacks, and, along with the anthropological claim of diminished intellect, justice became an untenable issue. How could justice be obtained by a people who were clearly inferior? Hence, the denial of justice had an anthropological justification.

So widespread has been the denial of basic human rights in education, criminal justice, health care, and wealth, that it has led

---

10. David Walker, *The Appeal to the Coloured Citizens of the World* (Baltimore, MD: Black Classic Press, 1993; orig., 1830), 33.

many a Black person to lament, "There is no justice—just us!" And sitting at the core of this mindset is the inability of whites to analyze effectively how this historic denial of Black people has produced white privilege—a mindset, no doubt, that is highly informed by the theological teaching that Christian faith is an individual phenomenon. As noted, in such a milieu, a liberating understanding of justice has little chance. The religious personalism of the early white church and its commitment to Black dehumanization have formed a formidable tandem wherein the very structure of the white church prevents it from developing a liberating approach to justice for Blacks. First, a personal religious approach cannot effectively inform a collective dilemma. Second, a personal religious approach that is collective enough to inform Blacks that the highest sin is not recognizing their subordinate status is self-serving and hypocritical. It is not prophetic but ideological.

This is why Black people can ill afford to allow whites to lead them to justice. If justice is to become a reality, Black people have to lead themselves. White pastors and theologians will eventually waffle on the issue of God's justice, hailing the virtues of frequent worship, prayer, and eternal life. This is sure to be followed by universalism, pointing to the goodness of a Lord who loves all the same, regardless of race, without taking into account that this only leads to an individualistic worldview. Furthermore, it conveniently does not take into account that Black suffering is far more distinct and disproportionate than white suffering and, more importantly, that white people are the source of that disproportionate suffering. A racist theology emphasizes only the distinctions between white people and Black people in every facet of human existence, while at the same time sweeping those distinctions under the rug before God. This is the mindset of a Pharaoh and not Moses, a Goliath and not David, a Herod and not Jesus.

This does not bring justice to the oppressed nor healing to the brokenhearted. It only says that justice does not exist for Black people, and they should accept it! It says that this is a white man's nation, and that is the way it will remain. Not only is it unjust; it is sinful. This is why, in practice, America really is one nation under God—a nation of white men! All others simply live here and reflect a cornucopia of races, nationalities, and even religious faiths, in principle, but do not share in the equality that a democracy promises. In sum, American justice is not blind . . . it has excellent sight and privileges white men. As such, it has no *vision*!

God, Oppressive Laws, and Justice

America's Christian leanings have been both a blessing and a curse for Black people. They have been a blessing in that the biblical emphasis on justice for the despised, despite white Christian leaders' interpretation to the contrary, provides a powerful base for a God partial to human equality. They have been a curse in that, precisely because of that racist interpretation, whites have come to understand the nation's laws to be the worldly extension of God's revelation—all of them! While this complementary relationship between America's laws and God's laws is what makes America "great" for many white Americans, it has meant for Black people a particularly hair-splitting engagement with the white power structure. For most whites, to obey the laws of America is synonymous with obeying God's laws.

Most recently, this theological approach became a source of national dialogue when then–Attorney General Jeff Sessions stated during a press conference that he saw no irregularities in the Trump administration's policy on separating families seeking immigration into the country. Sessions's rationale for defending the policy was that it is the responsibility of all citizens, and that "persons who violate the law of our nation are subject to prosecution. I would cite you to the Apostle Paul and his clear and wise command in Romans 13, to obey the laws of the government because God has ordained them for the purpose of order."[11] Those familiar with those words recognize the reference to the biblical passage Romans

---

11. "Attorney General Sessions Addresses Recent Criticisms of Zero Tolerance by Church Leaders," Fort Wayne, IN, June 14, 2018, https://www.justice.gov.

13:1. In essence, Sessions was arguing that the U.S. government is the secular arm of God and that if one does not want to lose the favor of God, then one would not violate a national law, for to do so is to violate divine law. It further assumes that all lawmakers in the history of America, namely, white and male, have created laws under the auspices of divine guidance, thereby claiming an additional orthodox legitimacy to those laws.

It is not difficult to see how this understanding of the law is extremely disconcerting for African Americans and other people of color. Even considering that white lawmakers were sincere in their work, the laws were formulated within a racist community that saw the denial of justice to Black people as a duty from God. This is because the lawmakers were being inspired by the God of white supremacy and not the God of Black liberation and why white lawmakers never considered that, because of their racist leanings, their construction of laws could be unjust. But most laws were and still are. For example, because the reduction to chattel and the enslavement of Black people were legalized by white political leaders, one was in violation of the law by attempting to escape slavery or to aid any slave seeking escape.

To further bolster their ability to keep slaves on plantations, the slave codes were adopted in every Southern state by white politicians with several levels of punishment for slaves caught escaping and those who aided and abetted their escape. The punishments were gruesome and macabre, ranging from branding, to the amputation of body parts, to burning at the stake. Furthermore, by law, slaves were to remain illiterate, were not to receive a formal education; they could not vote, could not pursue political office, were not to marry, and were not allowed to carry a firearm. By law, Black men could not be circumcised, and Black women could not be raped. The "promotion" to three-fifths of a person was only a self-serving gesture on the part of white southerners to increase representation in Congress in Southern states, but Black people still could not vote! The Fugitive Slave Act passed by white lawmakers in 1850 sought to return those slaves who had escaped to the North back to their owners, primarily because the law considered Black people the property of their owners and not human beings. In 1857, the Dred Scott decision, whereby the Supreme Court ruled that "a Black person had no rights that a white man was bound to respect," was informed by the Fugitive Slave Act.

Even after Emancipation, post-Reconstruction led to *Plessy v. Ferguson*, wherein separate facilities on the basis of race became legal and binding but overbearingly unequal! Separate but equal existed *de jure* but not *de facto*. Neighborhoods, schools, colleges and universities, parks, swimming pools, theaters, hotels, restaurants, retail outlets, interstate travel, amusement parks, beaches, courtrooms, cemeteries, and *churches* were all segregated, by law! This is why Black people could not easily accept this affinity between America's laws and God's laws. The God of biblical revelation created all humans in freedom and not in bondage to any other people. The proposition that bondage had to be embraced by Black people until the eschaton to find favor with God is both socially and theologically incongruent with the God of Jesus Christ. This is why Black people have constantly rebelled against their bondage and discovered through Jesus that God is most concerned with those in bondage. Slavery was not a divine institution but a racist institution.

> Slavery, in whatever point of light in which it is considered, is repugnant to the feelings of nature, and inconsistent with the original rights of man. It ought, therefore, to be stigmatized for being unnatural; and detested for being unjust.[12]

And so begins Black people's walk with American laws, which have been intentionally and inherently in opposition to the achievement and aspirations of Black people, making those laws unjust, and hence the reason why Black people have aligned themselves militantly against them. Amendments to the constitution were

---

12. Words of a writer by the pen name "Othello"; taken from Benjamin E. Mays, *The Negro's God as Reflected in His Literature* (Westport, CT: Greenwood Publishing, 1969; orig., 1938), 111.

added only through rigorous protest to grant Black people freedom from the slavocracy (Thirteenth), citizenship (Fourteenth), and the right to vote (Fifteenth). And even regarding the right to vote, the Fifteenth Amendment only gave Black men the right to vote, not Black women. That would not happen for another fifty years! Thus, Black people have rightly concluded that the best way to expose those laws as unjust was to break them and bring public scrutiny to them. Insurrectionists were hanged for planning escapes in contravention of the law, and protesters were jailed for violating segregation laws. Martin Luther King Jr. was arrested over one hundred times for violating segregation laws. He was not seeking to be an irritant to white people, but he was ardently seeking justice for Black people in a society in which the law was their biggest obstacle. This is why he often quoted Henry David Thoreau on civil disobedience: "In an unjust society, the only place for a just man is prison."[13]

There is both glory and danger in wedding divine laws to human laws. Whereas divine laws are unconditional and begin with God's love for humanity and creation, human laws are governed by environment and teaching from other human beings. Thus, having committed to a racist ethic that privileges white skin, it stands to reason that the laws created by whites would reflect a desire to preserve that privilege. When an evil such as racism guides the theology of Christian faith, the laws made by racist politicians, no matter how sincere, will also be racist. Because the God of Jesus Christ is a just God who governs as "no respecter of persons," racism is in violation of that God's will. Laws drafted primarily by white men for white men that only divide humans into communities based on race are in violation of the law of God. More importantly, to ask Black people to obey racist laws as they would God's laws is to ask Black people to accept a subordinate status in American life—it is to accept the place that the white community has prescribed. Tolstoy protests in a similar lament when he takes

---

13. Henry David Thoreau, *Resistance to Civil Government* (Prescott, AZ: Warfield Press, 2010; orig., 1849).

up the subject of obedience to contemporary laws in comparison to ancient laws.

> It was very well for the men of the ancient world to observe their laws. They firmly believed that their law (it was generally of a religious character) was the only just law, which everyone ought to obey. But is it so with us? We know and cannot help knowing that the law of our country is not the one eternal law.[14]

Is the question raised by Tolstoy the same with us in America? Are the laws of our country consistent with the God of Jesus Christ? Are those laws a true reflection of the God of Black liberation? I answer the question in the Black prophetic tradition, No! They continue to favor the white and the wealthy!

Thus, Black people have had to endure what those unjust laws have spawned, despite God's preference for the abused and humiliated. For white America has said to Black people that a free Black person is a contradiction in terms, for a Black person is neither human nor free. You have only two options—slavery or death! White people have been even more gruesome in executing public punishments on Black people for violating racist laws than in creating racist laws. Whether it be chopping a foot off for seeking escape from the plantation; cutting out a Black woman's fetus and shoving it in her mouth for insubordination; or castrating Black men, then shoving their testicles into their mouths and burning them on trees until they lie limp and become what Billie Holliday called "strange fruit"; or holding a knee on the neck of a Black man until he stops breathing in the process of executing "law and order"; or sending innocent Black men to the electric chair, whites have been as terrorizing as they have been wicked in flexing their strong arm of "justice." A man cannot but suffer when his whole life is defined for him by laws that he must obey under threat of punishment, though he does not believe in their

---

14. Leo Tolstoy, *The Kingdom of God Is within You* (Lincoln, NE: University of Nebraska Press, 1984), 121.

wisdom or justice, and often clearly perceives their injustice, cruelty, and artificiality.[15]

This is the essential difference in which an Attorney General Sessions and a Black American would view laws of governance. Because whites were never enslaved, segregated, discriminated against, lynched, raped, or denied the basic needs of survival, they have benefitted from laws of white privilege without taking into consideration how those laws adversely affect Black people. Sessions, along with other whites, is convinced that national laws benefit all citizens equally. And why? Because of the highly individualistic way in which Christian faith is practiced. It conveniently absolves whites of any wrongdoing in the creation of a "racist theocracy."[16] It styles systemic racism as a figment of the imagination and roots Black people's snail-paced progress in their lack of intellect, social skills, and industry.

So what does this mean? In the building of a racist nation, whites have been out of step with God from the nation's slave origins and have remained out of step in postslavery times. Furthermore, to create a thin line between those racist laws and divine laws and to pass off those laws as just and righteous represents a dangerous faith. By linking racist laws to divine laws, the authenticity of the approach becomes more credible, and, through multiple generations of teaching this linkage to children who then take it into adulthood, the task of Black liberation is made infinitely more difficult. Because whites are convinced that no law they have created has ever been unjust, they have been ever vigilant in defending the moral integrity, even the theological integrity, of those laws. In fact, the white way of life finds its sacredness in the presumption that all laws are just and benefit all equally, and are inspired by God.

This, however, is a false presumption. Equal justice has been a fraudulent constitutional claim, for it has been created by white people to normalize their privileged status but has no binding cul-

---

15. Tolstoy, *The Kingdom of God Is within You*, 122.
16. Harry H. Singleton III, *White Religion & Black Humanity* (Lanham, MD: University Press of America, 2012), 169–85.

tural or theological merit. But because they have had the power to realize that way of life, equal justice has been a slogan at best and a palliative at worst—neither of which aids the Black person in the struggle for justice.

As long as unjust laws continue to produce two Americas with their authenticity confirmed by their religious institutions, it diminishes the church's credibility and makes Christian theology an instrument of Black oppression rather than Black liberation. One America does not mean whites calling all the shots and Blacks accepting a comfortable place of subordination to whites. One America does not mean sacralizing racist wisdom that has rendered Black people subordinate. One America does mean sacralizing divine wisdom that proclaims the liberation of Black people. One America reflects a unity in policy that mutually benefits all and not just white people. Until that time, the God of Black liberation will continue to blaze the path of justice, letting Blacks know that they are free to challenge unjust laws that keep them in prisons, slums, poor schools, and low-paying jobs, and to call out the white Christian establishment for its sacrilegious patronage of state-sponsored bigotry.

Divine Justice and the Dispossessed

The path of justice has been potholed by *"the anatomy of Black containment."* Most notably, this has been achieved through the creation of the Black criminal. As Blacks have had to "steal away to Jesus" to secure intermittent freedoms, white America has been there at every turn to reconstruct racism to maximize white privilege. That criminality was inescapable because of the deprivation of basic human rights and the legality of racism itself. As we have already established, Black folks were fed the bare minimum, just enough to keep them alive and as functioning laborers. As stated earlier, to survive, slaves would often "steal" a chicken from the coop, or "appropriate" some pork earmarked for the big house and some vegetables from the garden (which they tilled and harvested) for more vibrant meals for their families. Criminal activity also occurred when slaves "stole away" to the North and to Canada to secure their freedom—a freedom that they were convinced God created them to have.

White leaders, especially religious leaders, would use this "propensity to steal" on the part of slaves to establish the claim not only that Black people were innate criminals, but, because of the violent insurrections of the early nineteenth century, that Black men, in particular, were dangerous and needed to be contained. When coupled with the white people's conclusions about Black people's dislike for themselves and obvious intellectual challenges, and their lack of any viable work ethic except at the point of a whip, a virulent Black male stereotype would begin on the plantation and make its way up to present-day views of Black men.

> They take us . . . and make us afflict each other as bad as they themselves afflict us—And to crown the whole of this catalogue of cruelties, they tell us that we the (blacks) are an inferior race of beings! Incapable of self-government!!—We would be injurious to society and ourselves, if tyrants should loose their unjust hold on us!! That if we were free we would not work, but would live on plunder and theft!!! That we are the meanest and laziest set of beings in the world!!!! That they are obliged to keep us in bondage to do us good!!!!![17]

These stereotypes were the foundation for the creation of an anti-Black society that whites presented as the best possible reality for Black people who, if free, would be clearly incapable of making sound decisions about their future. Seeing this, God, in God's infinite wisdom, has sent white people to Black people to control their natural impulses to slothfulness and lawlessness. It is, indeed, during slavery that the "law and order" mentality of whites was born.

But with the God of Black liberation ending slavery, whites regrouped and took the criminality argument through to post-Reconstruction and segregation. The need to "contain" Black men became an even greater priority, given their ability to now move

---

17. Walker, *The Appeal*, 85.

around and compete with white men for economic opportunities. That sense of containment was also driven by Black men's ability to have sex more freely with the daughters (and wives!) of white men. Hence, the sexual psychosis of white men had become official! Answering the call to white purity, with the publication of Robert Shufeldt's *The Negro: A Menace to American Civilization* (1907), Thomas Dixon's *The Leopard's Spots* (1902), and the movie *Birth of a Nation* (1915) by D. W. Griffith, these men argued that Black people's deficiencies were natural and that the worst thing that happened to them was emancipation. Furthermore, these publications laid the foundation for a virulent white supremacist's politics of rigid racial separation and our current criminal justice system.

In practice, though, it is more of a criminal *injustice* system, in which Blacks have been disproportionately sentenced and executed in comparison to whites. Thus, taking the criminal label of Black people out of slavery and modernizing it, white men regrouped and created a horrific criminal system with racists at all levels, from street cops to district attorneys, to federal judges and Supreme Court justices, in order to legitimate stereotypes and sentence Black men excessively to keep their communities "safe." Michelle Alexander, who has labeled this current trend to Black criminality as "the new Jim Crow," states:

> If and when crime rates rise—which seems likely if the nation's economy continues to suffer—nothing would deter politicians from making black and brown criminals, once again, their favorite whipping boys. Since the days of slavery, black men have been depicted and understood as criminals, and their criminal "nature" has been among the justifications for every caste system to date. The criminalization and demonization of black men is one habit America seems unlikely to break without addressing head-on the racial dynamics that have given rise to successive caste systems.[18]

---

18. Michelle Alexander, *The New Jim Crow: Mass Incarceration in the Age of Colorblindness* (New York: New Press, 2012), 240.

> In fact, the criminal justice system has become so obsessed with containing Black men that the notion of rehabilitating prisoners has fallen by the wayside in favor of holding areas simply to keep Black men out of the society. The system is no longer concerned with the inmate reform . . . only social control. It is no longer concerned with the prevention and punishment of crime, but with the management and control of the dispossessed.[19]

Alexander is aptly demonstrating that by engaging in a public display of power over the dispossessed, the making of a criminal *injustice* system is not just a historical issue but also a theological one! In structuring a society based on privilege, white people fail to realize that the very God who they think is fueling their society of white privilege, the God of Jesus Christ, is the same God who is fueling Black people's liberation struggle from the plantation to today. Even though second-class citizenship is what white lawmakers have prescribed for Black people, it is not what God has prescribed. This is why Black people have been as diligent in affirming their humanity as white folks have been in demonizing it. It has been Black people's way of claiming a distinct difference between what white folks say about them and what God has said about them.

The God who is fueling white supremacy is not the God of biblical revelation but the God of white privilege, an idol god who will ultimately be defeated at the altar of justice. The fact that the anatomy of Black containment has been informed by a pseudo-Christian perspective makes it especially earmarked for God's chastisement. But it is the God of Jesus Christ, the God of the dispossessed who dies and resurrects to ensure the victory of the oppressed—a God who has accompanied Black people from the ships to the streets; a God who fueled their freedom movements, revealing to them by God's own death on the cross to "steal" their freedom from their earthly masters, who have forfeited their right

---

19. Alexander, *The New Jim Crow*, 118.

to tell Blacks how to live—to steal away to Jesus, their eternal home; a God who informed them that their designation as criminals by whites was not their true designation. The white labeling of Black humanity had been nullified the moment they made Black people niggers, shines, and coons. Their white understanding of justice will always be challenged by Blacks as long as it is committed to the dehumanization of Blacks. The good news of the gospel is that the white understanding of racial justice will always be challenged by the God of Black liberation as long as it persists in imaging Black humanity in any way other than in the way God had created them. As Cone stated,

> As long as whites may pass laws against blacks, black people will affirm their dignity in spite of white racism at every opportunity. This country will continue to be two societies—one black and one white—as long as whites demand the right to define the basis of relationship.[20]

Black people find liberation in the reality that Jesus himself was considered a sinner and a criminal who fought for the lowly and despised, and against an extremely negative public image that was carefully crafted by his enemies. Thus, just as danger and cruelty were no strangers to Jesus, they are also no strangers to Black people. It is how their identifications mesh in the contemporary era. This is why they knew they could take their sufferings in the way of freedom to Jesus for he had firsthand knowledge of societal rejection.

Indeed, for the God of Jesus Christ, breaking the yoke of slavery and cutting the chains of oppression are the foundation of justice, not maintaining injustice as white folks would have Blacks believe.

Is not this the fast that I choose:
　to loose the bonds of injustice,
　to undo the thongs of the yoke,

---

20. James H. Cone, *Black Theology & Black Power* (Maryknoll, NY: Orbis Books, 1989), 146–47.

> to let the oppressed go free,
> and to break every yoke?
> Is it not to share your bread with the hungry,
> and bring the homeless poor into your house;
> when you see the naked, to cover them,
> and not to hide yourself from your own kin? (Isa 58:6–7)

Black people will not stop their quest for justice because they cannot. Propelled by a just God, they are perpetually in motion to the attainment of justice; and, although white racist measures may temporarily impede the Black quest for justice, they will never be able to completely kill the Black person's natural inclination to human freedom. This is because God created Black people in freedom, and because the cross was not the final answer on human destiny. But because Jesus lives, Black people can face tomorrow—an unknown set of occurrences and circumstances yet pregnant with unlimited possibilities for freedom and justice from a known God who loves Black people.

Black people have known, without the benefit of formal education and seminary training, that slavery, segregation, and discrimination are neither right nor just. They have certainly known that white supremacy is an inauthentic way of being human and contrary to being Christian. They know that the salvation and justice of the God of Black liberation are imminent!

6

The Path of Liberation

God is a liberator . . . and a liberator in the here and now! Nothing identified with human domination of one group over another can be reasonably equated with God. As the creator of all human beings, God loves them all equally. But because that equality is not reflected in the world, God reveals God's disdain with inequality. God loves liberation but hates oppression. God, in the freedom granted to human beings, even allows that oppressive context to form but at that point becomes a God of liberation, identifying the divine will with liberating those who are the victims of structural injustice. Because that identification is *in toto*, the reality of the oppressed becomes God's reality. The despised, stereotyped, vilified, and demonized reality of the oppressed becomes God's reality. Their humanity, or lack thereof, becomes God's humanity.

How do we know? God so identified with oppressed humanity that God became human not for the rich, the famous, or the monarchy but for a vilified and despised community; he was born in a manger as an unknown son of ordinary parents. The community's struggle became his life; his life became his ministry, and in his ministry lies the salvation of the world. When he began his ministry and commissioned his disciples, he did not engage in a universal ministry but directed it to those suffering most. He was clear with the disciples, when he sent them out into the world, "Go nowhere among the Gentiles, and enter no town of the Samaritans, but go rather to the lost sheep of the house of Israel" (Matt 10:5–6). Jesus was not interested in touting the virtues of a universal gospel. Since the Israelites were the people most in need of a healthy self-image and self-determination, God was concerned with helping a particular people deal with a particular problem of injustice that they could not overcome themselves. In short, having seen a segment of the human family encounter human oppression from another segment, God goes into liberator mode, effecting a return to the freedom in which God created all humans. As Gustavo Gutiérrez states,

> We know the Lord from his works; these make it clear to us, as we have now been reminded, that God liberates because God is a liberator, and not conversely, as we tend to think; that God does what is just because God is just; that God enters into covenants because God is faithful. God sanctifies because God is holy, and gives life because God is life, because God is what God is.[1]

As a liberator, God understood that a definitive statement had to be made to the world that could be best accomplished, first, by becoming human in Jesus, and, second, by becoming human to a poor community that had been systemically ostracized.

In Christian history, God has been referred to as the creator, comforter, all-powerful, all-knowing, perfect, healer, but the description that is often conspicuously missing from theological discourse is *liberator*. In other words, whatever else may be said about Christian faith, the realization of the promises of God, to be with the oppressed in their struggle for liberation, does not happen after physical death but is fulfilled in the here and now—and primarily in the concrete struggles of the disinherited in their quest for freedom. Gutiérrez notes,

> Christian faith is a historical faith. God is revealed in Jesus Christ, and, through him, in human history and in the least

---

1. Gustavo Gutiérrez, *The God of Life* (Maryknoll, NY: Orbis Books, 1991), 65.

important and poorest sector of those who make it up. Only with this as a starting point is it possible to believe in God.[2]

Gutiérrez makes clear that, in an oppressed context, adoption of a faith worldview is inextricably linked with a God of history or, more to the point, *a God who liberates in history*. As such, white Christian teachings about the primacy of a heaven after death have no place in God's plan for humanity.

Salvation is not an otherworldly phenomenon but a this-worldly realization of the divine will. To suggest otherwise is to plunge the liberation imperative into the social irrelevance that has come to define Christian theology for two millennia. However, just as Jesus brought a new covenant to first-century Palestine to tear asunder the established theology of his time, which sanctioned the status quo and taught the oppressed to endure their oppression, so too is God acting in contemporary history to empower the oppressed to tear asunder the established theology of our time—a theology that condones Black dehumanization, a theology that diminishes history in the liberation process. As Gutiérrez notes, "If we are to dwell in the tent that the Son has pitched in our midst, we must enter into our own history, here and now, and nourish our hope in the will to life."[3]

The liberation imperative emanating from Jesus does not provide us the luxury of being whisked away to heaven but demands that the liberating message of Jesus be brought to light here and now. Indeed, the good news of the gospel is that it is not a one-era gospel! It is relevant in every era and in every context where human oppression exists. Moreover, oppressed people can fully engage unbridled liberating activity, knowing that God has assured the victory over oppression through the resurrection. This is the true meaning of the resurrection—the overcoming of an oppressive death. The truth of the gospel is that the crucifixion represents the passion and death of an oppressed people who are resurrected not in heaven but on earth.

---

2. Gutiérrez, *The God of Life*, 85.
3. Gutiérrez, *The God of Life*, 85.

Our path of liberation begins with awareness of the victory of the Black struggle over white supremacy. Jesus's resurrection over "the troubles of this world" assures Black people of their liberation. The lynchings, castrations, rapes, gross racial inequities, police brutality, racial bigotry, and their Christian justification will not impede the destiny of Black liberation. The path of liberation requires us to debunk the legitimacy of Christian racism. In fact, the liberation imperative brings an end to racial bigotry. Racism is not of God but of the Antichrist insofar as it privileges whites to the detriment of Blacks. It undermines God's commitment to liberation and distorts faith by making Black people think that fighting against racism is ungodly. Moreover, racism shows its demonic hand by declaring white rule as the kingdom of God.

The path of liberation has been created by God. This world does not belong to white men alone but to all human beings. God did not intend for white men to hoard wealth and resources so that people of color live in substandard housing with meager public assistance. Therefore, because of racism, God comes as liberator to realize what white men have prevented in history—freedom, justice, and equality! And the fact that God's will has been used to justify that deprivation has only deepened God's liberating resolve. In the quest to identify with Black people who are oppressed for no other reason than their blackness, God takes on that symbol of oppression as God's oppression. No approach to Christian faith has relevance in our time unless it is grounded in Black liberation. Thus, to truly know God "means being on the side of the oppressed, becoming *one* with them, and participating in the goal of liberation. *We must become black with God!*"[4] In other words, becoming a true Christian, a true person of God, means embracing the God of Black liberation—a God who demands an abandonment of the old status-quo theology that has privileged white Americans and has sentenced Black people to the worst forms of physical and mental abuse in modern history.

---

4. James Cone, *A Black Theology of Liberation* (Maryknoll, NY: Orbis Books, 1990), 65.

As a result of the white way of life, Black people have experienced unimaginable horrors—all masquerading as ordained by God! But the God of Jesus Christ is not the God of white supremacy. The God of Jesus Christ is the God of Black liberation, hell bent on assisting Black people in the process of bringing down the curtain on racism. As Cone has noted,

> God's election of Israel and incarnation in Christ reveal that the liberation of the oppressed is a part of the innermost nature of God. Liberation is not an afterthought but the essence of divine activity.[5]

The heart of Christian faith is that God is an active God. This has already been identified by white theologians in distinguishing between the God of the Bible and the gods of Greek philosophy. But the real scandal of Christian faith is that God is active *as a liberator of the oppressed.* It was a scandal for the pundits of first-century Palestine who mocked Jesus for claiming he was the son of humanity, and it is a scandal today for a white Christian community that mocks Black people for asserting that the God of Black liberation has arrived.

The Spiritual Nature of the Liberation Struggle

Since God's essence is liberation, the movement from oppression to liberation is profoundly spiritual. Long separated from the liberation struggle by white Christian leadership, it is the Spirit who drives the divine imperative for liberation. When Jesus proclaimed that God demands "release of the captives," "sight to the blind," and "to set at liberty those who are oppressed," Jesus prefaced those directives by proclaiming, "The Spirit of the Lord is upon me" (Luke 4:18). Jesus is not only the liberation of humanity but the guiding force of the divine will. Nothing affirms the Spirit of God more than making right what human beings have made wrong—in this case, spiritually connecting with the oppressed in their struggle

---

5. Cone, *A Black Theology of Liberation*, 65.

by infusing in the oppressed the unquenchable desire for freedom and coming in history to an oppressed community to reveal the divine will to the world. In other words, the Spirit of God becomes real in the historical struggle for human self-determination. The practice of liberation is *necessary* for Christian life and, therefore, for the basic spirituality of that life.[6] God's liberation and God's Spirit are synonymous not only in their functionality but also in their primacy. Jon Sobrino notes,

> By its very nature, the practice of liberation today brings Christians face to face with ultimate realities, to which the spirit must respond with ultimacy. The precise manner of this response cannot be programmed. But it will obviously be in terms of a spirituality that *of its very nature* comes face to face with the ultimacy of reality.[7]

This "ultimacy of reality" comes in making right the wrong of oppressive relationships.

In our context, the God of Black liberation's identification with Black people is in their continuing struggle against white racism. For not only are we dealing with a context that calls forth the very Spirit of God in the creation of racism, an oppressive phenomenon, but also with the fact that white Christian leadership has misrepresented God as one whose Spirit is rooted in Black oppression—the diametric opposite of God's Spirit! Thus, walking the path of liberation lies in freeing the Spirit from white theology that has divorced the Black struggle from the spiritual life. White Christian spirituality is that of a pious individual who is soft spoken, meek, and who always speaks kindly of everyone. The true Christian spiritual person for them is one who is nonrevolutionary, nonengaging in issues of social justice, and who proudly absolves oneself from any social responsibility. Their spiritual perspective personifies the Puritan ethic that views the world as the locale for the ungodly and demands a righteous

---

6. Jon Sobrino, *Spirituality of Liberation* (Maryknoll, NY: Orbis Books, 1988), 30.

7. Sobrino, *Spirituality of Liberation*, 30.

withdrawal from an irrevocably sinful world. In sheer theological inconsistency, this model of spirituality is supposedly drawn from an image of Jesus who possesses all of the above qualities and, for good measure, is also white! It is here where spirituality and the Christ event are in need of serious reconstruction.

So significant is the link between liberation and spirituality that when God proclaimed through Jesus that "the Spirit of the Lord is upon me," God was affirming that God's Spirit was concerned with the "release of the captives," not their perpetuation, with "rendering sight to the blind," not keeping them ignorant about their destiny, and setting at liberty "those who are oppressed," not keeping them oppressed until the eschaton. Given that the theology of white supremacy equates God's will with the perpetuation of Black suffering, it missed the true meaning of the Christ event in its most significant aspect. Such a theology sought to create in Black people a Puritan disposition to serve the ends of white privilege more than the Spirit of God. White theology sought to instill in both Black and white Christians a meek, passive disposition on matters of social engagement, severing spirituality from the social, economic, and political realm of American life. The intent was to create a spirituality that was divorced from revolutionary/liberating activity and thereby maintain white privilege. Furthermore, it absolved white politicians of any responsibility for the unequal distribution of national resources. Yet with this decision, white men made one the most egregious errors in America's history, given that a nation's political deliberations are not just political. Indeed, if Jesus's proclamation holds true, then a nation's political deliberations also determine its spiritual condition. As the author, James Baldwin writes,

> Freedom is hard to bear. It can be objected to that I am speaking of political freedom in spiritual terms, but the political institutions of any nation are always menaced and are ultimately controlled by the spiritual state of that nation.[8]

---

8. James Baldwin, *The Fire Next Time* (New York: Dell Publishing, 1964), 120.

Baldwin rightly recognizes that no relevant treatment of spirituality can be constructed without ultimate concern for the oppressed and how prior political decisions have contributed to that oppression.

The hypocrisy in this discourse can hardly be ignored when we consider that racist political deliberations have been devoid of a spiritual check for centuries and undertaken by white men who are convinced of their *Christian* values. And therein lies the scandal of spirituality. The life and ministry of Jesus cannot be so summarily misrepresented for an eternity. Whatever one may derive from the Christ event, what cannot be derived is that, in an oppressive context, Black people are to accept their lot humbly until the end of history. Jesus was interested not in the old reality but in the new reality—one that would decisively transform the way in which oppressed humanity lives. Jesus was a revolutionary. He insisted, even to the cross, that human liberation is the Spirit of God, that we were created in that liberation, and that the eternal nature of God is embodied in that liberation. But he also knew that could not happen until the challenge to the old way of doing things, and the sure backlash that was to follow, began. Thus, the true meaning of the Christ event was to begin the Black struggle for the goal of human liberation. If in the human heart there is a capacity imprisoned, that human heart through the Spirit of the risen Christ can be released to a broader life.[9] In other words, the meaning of the Christ event will endure because the historical Jesus overcame death and became the Risen Christ. The Spirit is the overpowering force that liberates Black people from the theological quicksand of Christian racism, which has kept the human spirit mired in ritual and piety. This means that universal talk about "the goodness of the Lord" is not the ultimate spiritual goal. Rather, the goal is opening oneself up to God's liberating Spirit in commitment to Black liberation. Liberated personality is God's most successful

---

9. Benjamin E. Mays, *The Negro's God as Reflected in His Literature* (Westport, CT: Greenwood Publishing, 1969; orig., 1938), 81.

force, by which whole communities may be elevated from spiritual lethargy and transformed into resplendent life.[10]

In its true essence, spirit is communal. Because Black oppression is a communal phenomenon, it is a matter of ultimate concern for God. That is the good news of God on the path of liberation. Because the Spirit of God effectuates human liberation, and in this context, human liberation for Black people, the relevance of the Christ event is not that it is just a first-century event. It is *the* happening in the Christian world and the salvation of the entire world. The litmus test for true spirituality lies in one's work on behalf of the dispossessed and voiceless in the world. It does not reside in universal platitudes for those who are not able to make a break with "old wineskins." In fact, the path of liberation's major difficulty lies in the fact that white people have become so deeply entrenched in centuries of their own bigotry that they are not really capable of envisioning the radical changes needed to overcome the Black condition. We are reminded again by Baldwin, who writes,

> Now there is simply no possibility of a real change in the Negro's situation without the most radical and far-reaching changes in the American political and social structure. And it is clear that white Americans are not simply unwilling to effect these changes; they are, in the main, so slothful they have become, unable even to envision them.[11]

The path of liberation means taking on the evil of white racism in the ultimate irony—that whites have been sold a Christian faith of Black subordination to maintain their privilege and that white Christian leadership, the biggest obstacle to a liberated Black humanity, has presented a racist faith uncommitted to a new Black humanity. For invariably, "when the country speaks of a 'new' Negro, which it has been doing every hour on the hour for decades, it is not really referring to a change in the Negro, which

---

10. Mays, *The Negro's God*, 81.
11. Baldwin, *The Fire Next Time*, 114.

in any case, it is quite incapable of assessing, but only to a new difficulty in keeping him in his place, to the fact that it encounters him (again! again!) barring yet another door to its *spiritual* and social ease."[12] Another door has been barred from whites, in Baldwin's terms, because it is too busy with the politics of Black subordination and not the politics of Black liberation. Whites have treated spirituality as mainly individualistic and to the extent it has been treated in communal terms, God's will has been synonymous with white privilege not Black liberation. Consequently, they have equated Christian stewardship with "keeping Blacks in their place." This is a gross misunderstanding of the Christ event. As a practical corollary, most whites are miffed as to why Blacks continue to protest and scathingly critique their bigotry in a "post-racial" society, but seldom do whites acknowledge the privileged reality that Black subordination has accorded them.

What is not understood is that the continued power of Black people to challenge and to overcome white supremacy is the Spirit of God operating in their liberating activity. What whites fail to understand is that the Christ event is God fully aligned with and committed to the Black liberation struggle. As George Cummings notes,

> Freedom is God's freedom and is manifested in the persistent will of the oppressed to fight and kick against injustice and hopelessness. Jesus Christ is the crucified embodiment of God, who brings about black liberation by joining the black oppressed and sharing with them in the resurrecting power of the Spirit.[13]

The God of Jesus Christ is not a "law and order" God but rather an active participant in crafting a new law that sees the rage of Black

---

12. Baldwin, *The Fire Next Time*, 116.
13. George C. L. Cummings, "The Slave Narratives as a Source of Black Theological Discourse: The Spirit and Eschatology," in Dwight N. Hopkins and George C. L. Cummings, eds., *Cut Loose Your Stammering Tongue: Black Theology in the Slave Narratives* (Maryknoll, NY: Orbis Books, 1991), 65–66.

people as justifiable and channels it into liberating activity. As the recent uprisings across America in the wake of the "televised" executions of scores of Black men and women at the hands of police have shown, racial injustice will ultimately spawn racial unrest. Peace will never come as long as American law and order is not committed to listening faithfully to the unrest. The only way for peace to flourish is to liberate Black people. In other words, American law and order as we currently know them must be brought to an end and replaced with a new political reality that is consistent with the God of the Black experience. Cone states,

> It is impossible truly to hear the biblical story as told in the songs and sermons of black people without also seeing God as the divine power in the lives of the oppressed, moving them toward the fullness of their humanity. An ethic derived from this God, then, must be defined according to the historical struggle for freedom. It cannot be identified with the status quo.[14]

Given white privilege's commitment to the status quo, its political and theological structures cannot be a true expression of God's nature. That necessitates the coming of the God of Black liberation, who points out the evils of white racism and directs us to the divine purpose of the sociopolitical struggle.

The Sacred Nature of the Liberation Struggle

A distinct Black theology is indispensable for the path of liberation. This comes mostly from centuries of physical and mental mistreatment of Black people by white people. In other words, the God of Black liberation demands the development of a theology that speaks to the Black condition not as a means of perpetuating but of ending that condition. At the core of white theology is its assertion that there is a strict demarcation between the spiritual and the

---

14. James Cone, *God of the Oppressed* (San Francisco: Harper & Row, 1975), 200.

worldly. With this understanding, white Christian leadership was able to get Blacks to think that God was not interested in worldly affairs, and any attempt on the part of Blacks to appropriate God would be futile. To be sure, the intent was to destroy all sense of hope in a higher power who would help Blacks in their struggle for freedom. All other white theological axioms stem from this base. But slaves early in the institution were keenly aware of the oneness of spiritual and secular reality and found no substantive basis in white Christian leadership's claim of a separation between sacred and secular. As Cummings notes,

> The connection between their religious experience and the struggles of this world was, and is, a reaffirmation of the traditional African concept of the wholeness and integration of life. Religion was a dimension of life that pervaded every aspect of the slave community's life. Their "sacred" world was linked with their "profane" world.[15]

In fact, the sacred and the profane were one—there was no distinction. All reality was sacred.

Our challenge is owing to a distinct white theology that seeks a strict demarcation that emerged between the sacred and the secular in plantation life and is operative today. Its formidability lies in its universal presentation, which has galvanized more than a few Black and white Christians. The liberation imperative rarely makes its way into orthodox Christian language, because it is considered a historical rather than a Christian issue. This theological structure has allowed white intellectuals to promote a literary tradition of anti-Black animus with no liberating response from the Christian community. But the contradiction here lies in the fact that, even though there was a supposed demarcation between the sacred and the secular, it did not prevent white Christian leaders from developing theological systems to hammer away at Black humanity. The *imago dei* became desecrated in Black inferiority. In other

---

15. Hopkins and Cummings, eds., *Cut Loose Your Stammering Tongue*, 65.

words, Black people had a barrage of white Christian theological claims about their inferior humanity imposed on them to legitimate white superiority. Hence, each theological statement about Black inferiority meant conversely a theological statement about white superiority. This is a distinctive characteristic of white theology. It became so orthodox in the life of the church that it became known simply as "theology," but, in reality, it is "white theology." From Jesus's whiteness to the Bible's "ironclad" defense of slavery, to sanctuaries featuring buzzard roosts in balconies for slaves, to missionary conversions rooted in piety but not freedom, to carefully overseen "independent" Black churches to prevent insurrection, Christian theology committed itself to a white will to power rather than a Black path to liberation.

It became clear to Black people that they could not depend on white people to lead them to freedom. A new theological tradition was needed. That meant a return to the African tradition that saw no separation between the sacred and the secular. For the new Black militant tradition, writings condemning slavery, runaway missions in the middle of the night, walking out of a white Methodist church that refused Blacks the prayer altar, and creating the Underground Railroad were as significant in God's eyes as what was happening in church on Sunday morning. In an oppressive context, ritual is great; but liberating activity is better. Making a joyful noise was not confined to melodious choir voices during worship but the sound of feet moving on wooded grass as Black folks made their way "north!" Being moved by a spine-tingling sermon had to be coupled with the prophetic proclamation of a liberated Black humanity. Faith in God meant more than platitudes of endurance. It came to mean a singular preoccupation with the movement from the plantation to the promised land. A promised land in this world not beyond. Blacks understood, more importantly, that the God of white enslavement was not their God, and was not the God of Jesus Christ. By contrast, their God loves freedom and hates oppression and willed their liberation, not their enslavement. They understood that to truly praise God was to strike blows for freedom!

Militant Black leadership also understood that the God of the church was a white God committed to white bourgeois America and not to the Black community. Getting the God of Black liberation to shine forth was crucial in breaking the mesmerizing effect white religion had on Black people. If not, the Black liberation journey would be fatally compromised. This became evident when militant Blacks encountered Blacks who wanted to stay with Pharaoh and were convinced that the best possible reality for Black people was to live under white rule forever. Discovering this reality among Blacks irked abolitionist Frederick Douglass like nothing else.

> I have met many religious colored people, at the South, who are under the delusion that God requires them to submit to slavery, and to wear the chains with meekness and humility. I could entertain no such nonsense as this; and I almost lost my patience when I found any colored man weak enough to believe such stuff.[16]

Douglass is making the case for a new way of looking at God that lifts the conscience of Black people out of the abyss of white theology.

What developed from militant Black leadership was a distinct Black theology that consisted of two major pillars—excoriating white ministers and theologians for linking the God of Jesus Christ to Black dehumanization and reversing the brainwashing of Black people who had been seduced by proslavery orthodoxy. Only then could a Black theology emerge that gave Black people hope for freedom in this world. As Mays notes,

> The ideas of God are developed socially to convince white people that God did not will slavery, and to free the Negro's mind of the belief that God ordained it. The effort is to rob slavery of its religious sanction and at the same time to help

---

16. Frederick Douglass, *My Bondage and My Freedom* (New York: Miller, Orton, and Mulligan, 1855), 159. See also Mays, *The Negro's God*, 123.

the Negro to create within his mind a genuine integrity with respect to himself and a desire for freedom.[17]

David Walker, like Douglass, also expressed his disdain for white Christianity, referencing a God of freedom who had enlightened him to the theological tricks of the white community.

> Indeed, the way in which religion is conducted by the Europeans and their descendants, one might believe it is a plan fabricated by themselves and the *devils* to *oppress* us. But hark! My master has taught me better than to believe it—he has taught me that his gospel as it was preached by himself and his apostles remains the same, notwithstanding Europe has tried to mingle blood and oppression with it.[18]

Walker, here, identifies both dimensions of the new Black theology that is unashamedly concerned with the liberation of Black people. Black people, however, are not interested in replacing a white racist nation with a Black racist nation. The interest lies, rather, in charting a new path to Black humanity by proclaiming to the world the God of Black liberation's intentions for a genuine encounter between Black and white people.

Indeed, the God of Black liberation is on the scene today to proclaim the reign of liberation, despite the fact that Europe, as Walker puts it, "has tried to mingle blood and oppression" with the gospel of Jesus Christ. And that blood has survived slavery and its abolition and has continued to haunt the practice of Christian faith. It has been the task of militant Black leadership to make its way through the thicket of the path of liberation, engaging a church that is still mired in a static orthodoxy. For the white church, it has meant mainline denominational support for slavery, segregation, and religious polarization. It has taken pride in remaining staunchly committed to a theology of meaningless God-talk that does not get to the heart of Black oppression. Contribu-

---

17. Mays, *The Negro's God*, 124.

18. David Walker, *The Appeal to the Coloured Citizens of the World* (Baltimore, MD: Black Classic Press, 1993; orig., 1830), 55.

tions to favorite charities and "safe" biblical passages that avoid a reckoning with the way Black people are treated continue to be mainstays. An insidious political centrism, whether liberal or conservative, and an arrogant militarism masquerading as patriotism coupled with homophobia, Islamophobia, and Christian superiority are the linchpins of the postslavery orthodoxy of the white church. But more for our purposes, the white church does not in any way possess a path of liberation. Its leadership still finds difficulty accepting, even in a Christian paradigm, that they do not fit the description of "the least of these"; rather, the Black people they had deprived of God-given rights do. They have yet to understand their treatment of Black people as the way the Egyptians treated the Israelites. It is easier to maintain that God favored them as the "chosen people," when they defeated the British in the Revolutionary War and became a "free" nation. The facts of history, however, will not hold sway: Egypt is the conscience of the slaveholder; Israel is the conscience of the slave. It is the latter, not the former, where God's liberation is at work.

In sum, freedom for Black people has never been granted by the white political establishment, but Black people have had to fight for everything they have obtained. And it has been the white church that has sanctioned the social, economic, and political actions of white leadership while at the same time publicly embracing the separation of church and state. In short, the white church has continued to treat the dichotomy between the sacred and the secular as the cornerstone of Christian orthodoxy—in a nonliberating way.

The Black church, while intuiting that there is everything ungodly about their oppression, has yet to break free from the theological cue it has taken from the white church. It has not completely divorced itself theologically from the white church. Furthermore, it has not overcome the sacred–secular dichotomy. It tends to value praise, ritual, elaborate edifices, and personal accomplishment over the path of liberation. It continues to favor a white Jesus of individual healings and not a Black Jesus of societal transformation, a God of compensatory rather than historical efficacy. It has also been mired in the theological distractions of homophobia, Islamophobia, and Christian superiority and tends to equate Black progress with personal friendships with "good" white folks. It prides itself on a contemporary innovation that values contemporary Black gospel music and artists and a scrapped printed program for worship so that the "spirit" can have its way; but seldom does that spirit make its way to Black liberation. This is mostly because the dichotomy between sacred and secular compels the leadership of the church to see the liberation of Black people as a secular and not a sacred issue. Today, our task is clear. We must free the Black church from slave Christianity and call it back to the original teachings of Jesus, and we must liberate the Black church as an institution and restructure it so that it can become the center of the Black liberation struggle.[19]

Indeed, the key to the liberation of America is a liberated Black church. For that to happen, it must shed its sacred/secular dichotomy and embrace a theological perspective that is as opposed to white supremacy as it is concerned with spirited worship services. The church that Jesus commissioned to Peter was not one primarily concerned with a sacred/secular orthodoxy. First-century faith leaders actually criticized Jesus as a sinner and a religious charlatan for not conforming to their myopic image of the true religious adherent. Jesus was interested in a church that was as interested in humanity's social condition as it was its religious condition—a church that ministers to the whole human, not just its so-called spiritual condition, a church that makes no distinction between the sacred and the secular. This is crucial to America's and the world's salvation.

What is needed is more prophetic Black religious leaders who are not interested in maintaining their good relationships with white pastors or becoming the darlings of the Rotary, Kiwanis, and Lions clubs. What is needed are Black religious leaders who are ready to make a break with a white Jesus and a mythical heaven. We are

---

19. Albert Cleage, *Black Christian Nationalism: New Directions for the Black Church* (New York: William Morrow, 1972), 175.

in need of Black religious leaders who are ready to condemn the white establishment for its impotent response to its own bigotry, the impact it continues to have on young Black men in particular, and make it an intricate part of the church's language. This impact includes the racist criminal justice system, the resegregated school system, ongoing executions of Black people by police, and income inequality, all of which must become areas of major criticism in the life of the church if it is to be relevant today. In so doing, the cornerstone of a new theology of liberation will be laid.

God and the Language of Liberation

Given that the oppression of Black people is antithetical to God's will and has thus given rise to the God of Black liberation, the charge to the oppressed by God is never to abandon the language of liberation. In any oppressive context the pen (and the tongue!) is mightier than the sword! Throughout American history, Black people have produced outspoken leaders who have unsettled the onward march of white racism, including the white church's collusion with that racism. From Frederick Douglass, who on July 5, 1852, in a speech loudly chastised America for creating a day of freedom for themselves but not Black people who were still languishing in the earthly hell of human bondage, to W. E. B. Du Bois, who prophetically laid down the path of liberation when he wrote, "the problem of the twentieth century will be the problem of the color line," to Dr. King, who, the night before his assassination, maintained that God had given him the greatest gift of all, and that was a trip to the mountaintop to see the Promised Land, the language of liberation is crucial to the Black quest for liberation.

This is why whites worked so diligently to keep Blacks from a formal education. The fear is that it would produce eloquent orators who had the ability to lift the world out of its racial malaise, drum up enough support internationally to end racism and to usher in the day of true human liberation. Because the struggle for liberation of any oppressed people is also God's struggle for liberation, and because human speech is indispensable to a liberation movement, God used even the voices of illiterate Blacks to hammer chinks into the white armor of Black oppression. In fact, God was revealing to the world that the first step toward a liberation worldview was language announcing a new way of being human, of being a liberated world. As Will Coleman notes,

> While striving for social and political freedom, they also fought for linguistic liberation. Through narrative, folklore, spirituals, and so forth, African American slaves liberated themselves from having their voices silenced from illiteracy. In spite of this limitation in a society that glorified literacy, they created in their own metaphorical language "limitless" worlds we may appropriate into a contemporary black theology of liberation.[20]

In order to create a new reality, a liberated reality, therefore, a corresponding language was needed to articulate it to the world. The language of liberation became imperative to convey not only to whites that their rule would not endure but also to convey to fellow Blacks that the time had come to stop "shuckin' and jivin'" with racial bigotry, to "speak yo' mind" and to gear up to "run away and get north."

Through language, the limited world of slavery had now encountered the limitless world of freedom—a world of freedom in the here and now that God had revealed to them in both their fallenness and their limitedness. This is why they were able to articulate the tragedy and the triumph of their seeming hopeless condition. For, on the one hand, they proclaimed, "Sometimes I feel like a motherless child," and, "Why they crucified my Lord," but on the other hand, they coupled that with, "Trouble don't last

---

20. Will Coleman, "Coming through 'Ligion': Metaphor in Non-Christian and Christian Experiences with the Spirit(s) in African American Slave Narratives," in Dwight N. Hopkins and George C. L. Cummings, eds., *Cut Loose Your Stammering Tongue: Black Theology in the Slave Narratives* (Maryknoll, NY: Orbis Books, 1991), 101.

always," and "Steal away to Jesus." The genius of the burgeoning language of liberation is that it was able to utter the anguish of daily dehumanization and at the same time put forward faith in the day when freedom would come, the faith of both "the substance of things hoped for and the evidence of things not seen." They were able to see freedom not only with the eye of history but also with the eye of faith. And this was not the freedom of death and the otherworldly ascension but of the day when their children would be liberated, in this world. This was not by happenstance but was instilled in them, despite their linguistic challenges, by the God of Black liberation. In short, the omnipotence of God employed the voices of illiterate slaves to announce the advent of a new nation and world. To appropriate this reality is to engage the imagination in the revelation of a possible world and the advancement toward a new way of existing in this world.[21]

The fact that God would use illiterate persons may surprise some, but the fact that God would use those from among the oppressed to articulate the new covenant in a racist America should not be surprising. For only those who have experienced the pain and suffering of human oppression are best qualified to speak to its effects. God would not choose someone white to lead Black people to freedom inasmuch as they have no experiential base to articulate the impact of racism on Black people. Moses, Aaron, David, Solomon, Samson, and the prophets were all commissioned by God from among the Israelites to lead them to freedom. More importantly, the new covenant was brought to the world by God through the incarnation into an oppressed and despised community. In that decision, God spoke from the standpoint of the oppressed and marginalized not only for first-century Palestine but for the world. Because Jesus was one with the poor and the oppressed, and God and Jesus were one with each other, God is one with the poor and oppressed.[22] That God identified directly with the voiceless

---

21. Hopkins and Cummings, eds., *Cut Loose Your Stammering Tongue*, 101.

22. Cone, *God of the Oppressed*, 31.

would hold true for any future generations of oppressive contexts and was also making a statement about the primacy of liberation in those oppressed contexts. In other words, God became the mediating liberator, taking on the suffering of an oppressed people to bring ultimate urgency to their condition. No conclusions will suffice that do not describe who Jesus was, what he did, and what he said as the direct expression and implementation of God in action, doing "divine things humanly," among Black people and on their behalf. When God sees us and meets us and judges us, are we being seen, met, and judged by a God who has actually experienced and now knows, at the lowest human level, what it means to be human?[23] Indeed, the God of Jesus Christ has become the God of Black liberation, effectuating divine liberation, first, by identifying with Black pain and suffering, and, second, by raising up a continuous line of Black voices to articulate God's presence in their struggle for liberation.

The language of liberation as evidenced in Jesus was both a language of comfort but also of what Kaj Munk calls a "holy rage" about the condition of the oppressed. This is why, on the one hand, Jesus said to the woman who touched the hem of his garment that his physical presence was not necessary to her being made whole as long as she had faith in God, and why she took comfort in his reply, "Your faith has made you whole." But on the other hand, this is also why Jesus kicked over the table of the money-changers in the temple and referred to the Pharisees as a "brood of vipers," even reminding them, "You are of your father, the devil." Laden in both statements is the new paradigm for a liberating language that has endured to the present day and will continue until liberation is achieved. It is a language that comforts the oppressed and condemns the oppressor. It is a language that intentionally makes a sharp distinction between good and evil. But more importantly, it is a language that makes clear that divine being is not neutral in human affairs. God made this explicit not simply by speaking

---

23. Major J. Jones, *The Color of God: The Concept of God in Afro-American Thought* (Macon, GA: Mercer University Press, 1987), 93.

through a prophet but by becoming human and dwelling among the oppressed. In this sense, this is how the incarnation changed God.[24] It transitioned God from a God who prepared prophets to a God who became a living, oppressed human being. In other words, God, in taking on oppression, was revealed to the world as a liberator.

Thus, embodied in Jesus is the ultimate language of liberation: "I am the way, and the truth, and the life. No one comes to the Father except through me" (John 14:6). By using God's omnipotence to demonstrate to the world that death need not worry the oppressed, God was making the initial utterances of the language of liberation. God was saying that the process of liberation is not just a historical happening; it is a divine happening. "I am the resurrection and the life" (John 11:25).

Given that life takes on death and ultimately overcomes it, those living in death-like conditions and who are subject to random acts of violence, and who live constantly at "tip-toe stance" now realize that they are free to act in accord with God's liberation imperative. They now know that God has created a path of liberation that will reach its destination. This means that Black people can now "tell it like it is," without fear of white rejection, ridicule, and branding in the media as iconoclasts, racists in reverse, opportunists, demagogues, or devils incarnate. This is the language of racists who want to preserve "the white way of life." But because the God of Black liberation has arrived, Black people can now fully possess the linguistic liberation that God has granted, knowing that white proscriptions on their humanity may endure for a season but cease when "morning" comes! Black people can now castigate white religion and a white Jesus as the Antichrist and deal with the consequences knowing that they are on the path of truth, the path of liberation—a path created by God so that oppressed voices can proclaim their unquestioned right to be free.

By becoming incarnate in the Word, as the Gospel of John begins, the Word is the divine element in the universe that con-

---

24. Jones, *The Color of God*, 93.

demns oppression and convicts the voiceless. In the end, it is not what white folks say about Black humanity that is true but what the bearer of truth—Jesus—says!

> The Father, and the Holy Spirit are not the Word. God and the Word are not the same, but they must be taken together (with the Holy Spirit), as a unity, if they are to explain God in the fullness of his being. God is at one with his Word, because his "Word" is communication of his being.[25]

This is how the Christ event changed humanity! By empowering oppressed people with a Word that would liberate in contexts of oppression, God was identifying God's Spirit with the struggles of the oppressed and made God's intentions known to the world that God's will prevails in human affairs. God has revealed to the oppressed community that the Spirit of liberation is the essence of divine being. In so doing, God reduces white claims of eternal bondage to distortion and provides Black people with the "untimely" language to challenge white rule with every fiber of their being—even unto death. And even unto death, Black people can rest easy knowing that they have taken one last shot at the stench of bondage and its "perfect hatred."

> *Make me a grave where'er you will,*
> *In a lowly plain, or a lofty hill;*
> *Make it among earth's humblest graves,*
> *But not in a land where men are slaves.*[26]

Black people have been given the linguistic privilege of hammering away at white supremacy in "Word" and in deed with the assurance that a future generation of Black people will reap the benefits of multigenerational struggle and be totally liberated in this world. This is why God inspired Dr. King on the night before his assas-

---

25. Jones, *The Color of God*, 96.
26. Frances Ellen Watkins Harper (1825–1911), "Bury Me in a Free Land," https://poets.org/poem/bury-me-free-land. See also Mays, *The Negro's God*, 120.

sination in Memphis to say, "I may not get there with you but we as a people will get to the Promised Land." The "Promised Land" was not in the hereafter for Dr. King but in this world—the same land in which white supremacy was formed! Fear had been totally removed by the God of Black liberation—the God whom King had encountered in the faith of his foreparents even unto the last "Word" of his public career: "I am not fearing any man. Mine eyes have *seen* the glory of the coming of the Lord."[27]

Black Liberation and the Salvation of the World

The path of liberation is paved by God for the oppressed, in whose liberation the world is transformed. God has chosen freely to intervene in the struggle of Black people and has chosen to intervene for their liberation. Thus, even in hopelessness, one will find the hope of the world emanating from oppressed existence, seeking only freedom and not revenge on whites for what they have done and continue to do to Black people. This is not by chance. For not only has God intervened to liberate Black people; God has also instilled in Black people no compelling desire for retribution. Black people have left that to God. Oppressed Blacks and other people of color are the only signs of hope for the creation of a new humanity in America.[28] In creating such a path of liberation, God is demonstrating true grace and a salvation less concerned with a church member's destiny and more concerned with the destiny of the oppressed!

The first dimension of salvation along the path of liberation is that white theology has been too consumed with otherworldly salvation for the religious individual and not with the movement from oppression to liberation. Consequently, salvation has been distorted by white Christian leadership. Reformer Martin Luther, even in his religious sincerity, could see the danger in the monastic

---

27. Martin Luther King Jr., "I've Been to the Mountaintop," last speech of Martin Luther King Jr., April 3, 1968, at the Mason Temple (Church of God in Christ Headquarters) in Memphis, Tennessee.

28. Cone, *God of the Oppressed*, 221.

life and rightly concluded that God's grace should send us not to the monastery but to the world; yet, he could not see the danger of not extending that grace to peasant oppression, seeking instead a grace singularly interested in church reform. While the church has maintained an incomparable position in matters divine, that position was not just to point the path of individual salvation but to use its respectability to announce God's concern for peasant-like conditions. The church was not commissioned either to take no action on the condition of the voiceless or to brand peasant strivings for freedom as subversive. The Reformation, therefore, was a church reformation and not a human reformation! While the Catholic Church saw the need for a functional social teaching, it was only with assistance from Latin American liberation theologians that it was able to see that it was more consumed with excommunicating heretics (such as Luther), denying women the priesthood, and stressing the merits of confession than with a "preferential option for the poor."

A more effective understanding of salvation is through a this-worldly significance for the oppressed. For it is the liberation of the oppressed that holds the key to the world's salvation! When God made the decision to be a God of human liberation in the recognition of humanity's inhumanity to humanity, God was unleashing grace on a sin-sick world for its salvation. This did not mean a final judgment for the "new flesh" at the end of the world but rather the redemption of the world through the liberation imperative. This is why Black people have been so spiritually connected to God, despite white treatment and racist teaching. And that spiritual connection has not been simply a longing for the next world but a liberating destiny in this world.

God has revealed that grace in the sacrifice of Jesus on the cross. By giving up God's own son, who "came to set at liberty those who are oppressed," he was indicting the world in its creation of oppressive relationships, knowing that in its racist condition it would send Jesus to the cross. But the genius of God's grace is that God let him go to the cross, and even die on the cross. For what purpose? God was showing the world that God was committed to a new humanity through Jesus's life and that Jesus's death does not have the final say on the path of liberation. Rather, that final say holds that God's grace is fulfilled in Jesus overcoming the power of death as a paradigm for the oppressed overcoming the power of its social, economic, political, and theological death! This paradigm is the quintessential matrix for demonstrating God's commitment to a liberated humanity.

Through Jesus's resurrection, Black people have found "a friend in Jesus," who leads them to liberation in a hostile world. More importantly, the resurrection informs Black people that God is primarily interested in their liberation as God's own liberation. This is the meaning of God's grace in contemporary America. As Cone explains,

> On the cross, God encounters evil and suffering, the principalities and powers that keep people in captivity; and the resurrection is the sign that these powers have been decisively defeated, even though they are still very active in the world. But the victory in Jesus' resurrection is God's liberating act that makes possible human reconciliation with God.[29]

The second dimension of salvation along the path of liberation means using your body, mind, and spirit as living sacrifices in the Spirit of Jesus to liberate the oppressed. The fact that Jesus read that proclamation of his ministry in his home synagogue is a testament to the significance of the house of worship in the movement from oppression to liberation. Yet, we have lost sight as to why that is the case. God's grace extends to us the fight for liberation knowing that the cross is not the end of the path of liberation. Neither does that grace call us to link the Christ event with human oppression and certainly not to link Jesus's ministry with personal fulfillment. Rather, the church should be the preparation ground for those who commit themselves to the path of liberation. God's grace means that Black people can now fully engage the forces of white supremacy undeterred by white violence, backlash, and

---

29. Cone, *God of the Oppressed*, 236.

the refusal to enforce laws that should protect Black people. Black humanity can now be free to construct a new worldview in the spirit of Jesus's new covenant, which makes the liberation imperative the central dimension of Christian faith. It is a liberation imperative that extends not only to Black Christians but, because blackness is the meaning of oppression in contemporary America, extends also to all Black people, regardless of religious affiliation or none at all! Thus, God's grace is the gift to Black people to fight for their liberation, knowing that those who die will become martyrs and that Black people have in God the ultimate co-determining partner. Cone states,

> We have been given the gift of freedom to fight with God in the liberation struggle. We can now be reconciled with God because he has removed the conditions of alienation as represented in the powers of evil.[30]

In other words, the powers that are still functionally in control are not spiritually in control. God's grace reigns supreme in the eyes of the oppressed, and God's power will ultimately overcome the power of evil. This is why slaves said with unbridled enthusiasm, we are not going to "die no mo," and, "So my dear chillens don' yer fear." This is why the path of liberation contains freedom fighters so consumed with liberation that there is no place for fear in their spirits.

> There is no need to fear the earthly white power structure. Since Jesus, through Moses, led the exploited Israelite people to victory and finished off Satan with the Cross and Resurrection, no human advocates for the Devil could defeat Jesus' just cause of black people's struggle for liberation.[31]

This is why the salvation of the world is unintelligible in our time apart from the Black liberation struggle.

---

30. Cone, *God of the Oppressed*, 236.
31. Hopkins and Cummings, eds., *Cut Loose Your Stammering Tongue*, 21.

7

The Path of Eternity

The path of eternity is the most crucial path in the liberation of Black people. It is the path that realizes the kingdom "on earth as it is in heaven." It is a *coming* kingdom, in the process of being constructed, and, because of the resurrection, it is assured of realization.

The fact that the kingdom is a coming reality and not already in our midst is important for our purposes. Since the beginning of slavocracy, white Christian leadership has been preaching that the kingdom is at hand. The kingdom of white Christian leadership had already been formed through Black enslavement and had supposedly made salvation possible for Black people. And so began the realization of a kingdom whose eternity was rooted in Black enslavement.[1] White Southerners were even convinced, despite

---

1. See Charles Colcock Jones, *The Religious Instruction of the Negroes in the United States* (Savannah, GA: Thomas Purse Publishing, 1842); Walter Rauschenbusch, *A Theology for the Social Gospel* (Nashville, TN: Abingdon Press, 1990; orig., 1917); George Kelsey, *Racism and the Christian Understanding of Man* (New York: Charles Scribner's Sons), 1965; Eugene D. Genovese, *Roll, Jordan Roll: The World the Slaves Made* (New York: Vintage Books, 1972); Albert Raboteau, *Slave Religion: The "Invisible Institution" in the Antebellum South* (New York: Oxford University Press, 1978); Katie Canon, "Slave Ideology and Biblical Interpretation," in Katie Geneva Canon, *Katie's Canon: Womanism and the Soul of the Black Community* (New York: Continuum Press, 1995); James W. Perkinson, *White Supremacy: Outing Supremacy in Modernity* (New York: Palgrave Books, 2004).

being outnumbered by the Union army in the Civil War, that God would be with them in their defense of "civilization" and that their kingdom would not be torn asunder by liberals and troublemakers. They had been persuaded by their pastors and theologians that God was on their side. God's favor toward them would be so apparent that every eye was going to see that their civilization and the kingdom were one and the same.

Yet the facts of history and the integrity of biblical revelation do not allow such a close affinity. No kingdom can realize itself *in a context of bondage*! Such a claim makes a mockery of God's activity in the world in that it makes no distinction between the divine will and human oppression. In fact, the sweep of the biblical canon demonstrates a quest for the redemption of humanity through the ending of bondage in every way. The affirmation of a kingdom that covets bondage is diametrically opposed to the liberating message of the gospel. Yet the kingdom of white privilege has operated under the delusion that it could truly extract peace from a context of bondage—a peace that entailed getting Black people to gracefully accept the subordinate lot that God had supposedly bestowed on them. This is how white colonists understood civilization and the meaning of the kingdom.

But this is not the kingdom. The kingdom is still coming. It has yet to arrive. It demands the freedom of all humans—their original nature in creation. Any attempt to equate the kingdom with human bondage is antithetical to the divine will and does not faithfully honor the coming kingdom. That coming kingdom has nothing to do with making Black people eternal slaves or inferiors, which is also anti-Christian and anti-God. Thus, what white ministers preached as the kingdom became nothing more than a declaration of war against God. In so doing, America became the battleground of good and evil, right versus wrong, freedom versus slavery, Black liberation versus white supremacy.

Not only is white supremacy not the kingdom, it is also the height of theological contradiction. This is evidenced in the macabre acts of violence by whites to hold on to power and to paint Black strivings for freedom as ungodly. Because the kingdom is always on the move, it is not interested in freezing history by legitimating the status quo in God's name. If that were the case, the kingdom could never be realized. J. M. Coetzee made this clear in his novel *Waiting for the Barbarians*, as the "Empire" put forward a moral framework that branded their neighbors as barbarians for not recognizing the permanence of their inferiority in perpetuating the "Empire's" existence.

> Empire has created the time of history. Empire has located its existence not in its smooth, recurrent spinning time of the cycle of the seasons but in the jagged time of rise and fall, of beginning and end, of catastrophe. Empire dooms itself to live in history and plot against history. One thought alone occupies the submerged mind of Empire: how not to end, how not to die, how to prolong its era.[2]

It is for the same reason that whites have tried to maintain white privilege and resorted to every means of chicanery and outright enforcement of unjust laws or lack of enforcement of just laws to keep Black people in a state of subjugation. It is also why the "rule of law" and the carrying out of "law and order" have been key phrases of white people throughout America's history. It is also the reason why white privilege cannot in any way be associated with the kingdom. The purpose of law enforcement in this country's history has not been to enforce the law justly but to contain Black people—contain the "barbarians"! That is not the presence of peace; it is the absence of justice! What has been on trial in the American democratic experiment has not been the innate criminality of Black people but the immoral, social, and theological precepts of white people. Gustavo Gutiérrez draws a similar conclusion regarding the ruling class in Latin America.

> Theirs is an intolerance that does not fear even to commit murder when they see their privileges questioned and the dis-

---

2. J. M. Coetzee, *Waiting for the Barbarians* (New York: Penguin Books, 1982), 153–54.

honesty of their religion exposed. God is not with religious leaders who betray their task nor does God give them backing. The blood of Jesus can seal the new covenant, which he inaugurates because he dies as a just man at the hands of those who refuse to accept the God of life whom he preaches.[3]

Such governance cannot provide adequate vision on the path of eternity; it will only lead to the furthering of a "civilization" that has meant death for Black people. Such a "civilization" stands in contradiction to the God of life—the God of Black liberation. The God of white privilege is an idol god of history and not of eternity. Thus, the white kingdom is a kingdom that never was.

The coming kingdom, however, is rooted in the God of biblical revelation. It is the kingdom that does not demand passive acceptance of oppression but active engagement against it. Death is not the final answer, but life is. And life is the final answer in history—not the afterlife.

The coming kingdom is both undergirded by and permeates God's eternal reign of liberation. This is why the coming kingdom is the authentic kingdom of biblical revelation and not the already-realized kingdom of white privilege. The white kingdom is on its way to destruction before a just God, who is determined to free Black people. This is why the kingdom could not have been prepared by the God of white supremacy who is interested only in things as they are. The God of Black liberation's immutability lies in God's unchanging nature for change—God's unchanging thirst for Black freedom. The God of white supremacy is committed to the perpetuation of Black suffering and provides Christian sanction for that suffering. The God of Black liberation, however, is committed to ending Black suffering and takes seriously "the Spirit of the Lord" as that which brings life to a dead people.

Death has been the constant mainstay for Black people in the kingdom of white privilege, whether it be physical, mental, moral,

---

3. Gustavo Gutiérrez, *The God of Life* (Maryknoll, NY: Orbis Books, 1991), 73.

or spiritual. But "the Spirit of the Lord" brings the true kingdom and turns death into life for the oppressed. As Gutiérrez notes,

> The various human situations . . . (poverty, captivity, blindness, oppression) are all manifestations of death. The preaching of Jesus, who has been anointed Messiah by the power of the Spirit, will cause death to withdraw, by introducing a source of life that is meant to bring history to its fulfillment. This programmatic passage, therefore, confronts us again with the dilemma: death or life, which is central to biblical revelation and calls upon us . . . to make a radical choice.[4]

The dilemma that white planters have created from the inception of the colonies has been death or life, white supremacy or Black liberation, civilization or the kingdom. That has been the rallying cry of Black people from the time the first slave ships sailed across the Atlantic; but, unbeknownst to whites, it has also been the rallying cry of God. For the Spirit of God is life, not death. God chose life out of nothingness and allowed it to be. It is the choice that God also expects members of the human family to make with one another. White supremacy has not chosen life. It has chosen death for Black people and other people of color, using Christian faith as a pretext to connect that death with God's reign. It is for this reason that the God of Jesus Christ became the God of Black liberation. By becoming one with the Black experience, God was committing God's essence to the Black struggle for liberation.

The radical choice is the choice between the existing kingdom (white supremacy) and the coming kingdom (Black liberation), between history as it has been defined by white racists and history as it has been defined by the God of Jesus Christ. The former history demands that Black people be shells of human beings, marionettes for a system of injustice that has denigrated their bodies and continually dismisses their aspirations to freedom as inconsequential. But the history of the coming kingdom rewrites the narrative of white privilege by fully humanizing Black people. It

---

4. Gutiérrez, *The God of Life*, 73.

literally outlasts white privilege in its eternity and has enlisted the Black struggle for freedom as its fiercest advocate. It is that eternity that enables the kingdom to defeat a racist history and replace it with a liberated history. It is the meaning of eternity breaking in to history and giving history its spiritual nature and revealing God's intention for humanity. While God gives every human the choice of embracing the current kingdom or the coming kingdom, God's choice is clear: "I came to set at liberty those who are oppressed!"

History as the Venue of the Coming Kingdom

Racist power contains no spiritual dimension that will allow its existence until the end of history. Eternity breaks into history on behalf of the disinherited, not the bourgeoisie, for liberation not bondage. Therefore, eternity becomes the nemesis of history—its superior foe—that paradoxically realizes itself in history. It liberates history from itself and makes it the venue of liberation. It brings an eschatological "yes" to a history that has been possessed by an eschatological "no" to human liberation.

This is why slavery and postslavery racism were never the kingdom. They were unable to square their bourgeois commitments with a gospel that prides itself on changing history for the least of these—the despised, the lowly, and the abused. This is what happens when greed distorts civilization and makes it the cornerstone of racial imperialism. Furthermore, when greed distorts civilization, history becomes immoral because it becomes oppressive; it becomes the venue of denial of human freedom and the venue of constant attempts to normalize that denial. As Berdyaev has noted,

> There is nothing more trivial and banal than the defense of the blessings of civilization by the ideology of the bourgeois classes. These classes are fond of thinking of themselves as those who bear civilization forward and of contrasting themselves with the inward barbarian, by which they commonly mean the working class. They are afraid of the proletarian, because the proletarian means a being from whom all the

blessings of civilization and all the values of culture have been taken away.[5]

That "inward barbarian" in this context has been Black people whom, out of fear, whites subjugate to the worst and most virulent stereotypes that become internalized by both white and Black people. In addition to the stereotypes, Black people have received the least pay and still have not been compensated for two-and-a-half centuries of chattel slavery, even though slave owners have been compensated for relocating. And even in a postslavery context, criminality has become another venue of stereotype designed to make the public think that Black men, in particular, are a collective menace to American democracy without conveniently taking into consideration America's colossal crimes against Black, brown, and red humanity.

> This is the problem of crime, which is always, if not actual, at least potential, murder. Murder is committed not only by gangsters; murder is committed in an organized way and upon a colossal scale by the state, by those who are in possession of power, or by those who have only just seized it.[6]

With the power to control images and the political distribution of wealth, bourgeois values have guided the white flight to untouchable affluence. This is why there has been such an incessant effort by whites to distance themselves socially from Black people. Segregation, for example, meant legal separation but acutely unequal treatment—a trademark of bourgeois society! Yet, at the same time, Black people had to be kept close enough for whites to benefit from their labor! Thus whites were able to create the illusion of one society when there were really two: they were able to create the illusion of liberty and justice for all when there was really only justice for white people; they were able to create the illusion of one education system when there were really two; they

---

5. Nikolai Berdyaev, *Slavery and Freedom* (New York: Charles Scribner's Sons, 1944), 119–20.
6. Berdyaev, *Slavery and Freedom*, 119–20.

were able to create the illusion of one criminal justice system when there were actually two. In short, they were able to create the illusion of good will when in essence there was a hostile ill will that has always guided white interaction with Black people. Whether it is the quick misplacing of a home-equity application or a "denied" stamp on a voter registration application due to the inability to guess the correct number of jelly beans in a jar, or a public lynching attended by thousands of whites cheering in unison when a Black man is dangling mutilated from a tree, or a stoic white police officer casually staring down the street seemingly unaware or uninterested in the fact that his knee is on a Black man's neck while that Black man is uttering in the most strained voice, "I can't breathe," white hostility toward Black people has been a trademark of American history. It is the worst expression of humanity to humanity, seeking to court the illusion of progress, while doggedly clinging to unquestioned privilege, and to freeze history in racist conventionality.

But the highest illusion is that the God of the white community cares about all humans when their God really cares only about white people. This is certainly not the God of Jesus Christ. It is a God who glorifies a lack of accountability by whites in their interaction with Blacks. It rarely, if at all, calls whites to conscience about their treatment of Black people and is always looking to assuage white guilt for the insidious racial caste that whites have created in America. In short, it makes whites think that they are engaged in salvific behavior that is supposedly beneficial for both races but, in reality, is beneficial only for whites. This is mostly because whites are guided by their privilege and wealth. This becomes particularly clear in its theological constructions. Guided by a love of affluence and wealth and committed to doing whatever is necessary to maintain them, white Christian leaders do not possess the ability to legislate and theologize in a liberating mode. In other words, they are only able to deliberate about the future of the nation within a context of privilege. As such, they are unable to let history reroute itself to its liberated end. It sounds good in principle, but, when it comes to practical creation, there has been resistance every step of the way. Black people have procured the measures of freedom that they have despite white animosity and not because of white goodwill. In short, white Christian leaders cannot see the liberating grace of the gospel in its purest essence. They have been too controlled by history to allow eternity to enter history. For eternity's entry into history means a transformation in the racial dynamic to Black liberation and not a continuance of the existing situation permeated with their bigotry. It means a complete turnaround, a new way, if you would, in the treatment of Black people. This is not a dismissal of whites but an honest assessment, given that anti-Black animus has been a consistent part of white DNA for over four centuries. This is why Black people must never think that white people will liberate them. They can help at strategic points, but they cannot engineer the process. Deception of sincerity in helping the Black cause is too much of a chance for Black people to take. Whites are too committed to Black oppression to see authenticity in Black strivings for justice. White reaction to racial protest bears witness to that commitment.

We need to head history in a new direction, one that has the power to reroute our current history and eventually overcome it. That is the hope embodied in the gospel and how the suffering of Jesus on the cross is parlayed into a salvation that liberates the human family—a hope seen in the suffering and blood of Black people, in the affirmation of their humanity, and in a world that has sought to decimate it at every turn. In this regard, there is a historic parallel between the *unmerited* suffering by Jesus and Black people and also, paradoxically, between the *merited* suffering by Jesus and Black people. On the one hand, the suffering is unmerited because there is no prior oppressive treatment by Jesus or Black people to justify the retributive suffering of either. On the other hand, there is a merited suffering in sacrifice by both inflicted by insecure power agents seeking to maintain a racial and religious status quo. Thus, merited suffering, as I term it, is more of a sacrificial suffering taken on by Jesus and Black people that not only has the power to liberate Black humanity but is the medium by which the salvation of all humans is made possible. In other words, both Jesus and Black people have been crucified for the sake of humanity's freedom. And it is that paradigm of God entering history with the eternal dictum of liberation that emboldens Black people to not only push the envelope but, in the spirit of Jesus, to kick over the damn table in the temple and run away the money-loving leadership. In the mystery of God's revelation, Black Christians believed that just knowing that Jesus went through an experience of suffering in a manner similar to theirs gave them faith that God was with them, even in their suffering on lynching trees, just as God was present with Jesus in suffering on the cross.[7] It is the power of the blood—a blood that never loses its power, the blood on Jesus's hands and feet, the blood on Black people's backs from merciless whippings, and blood flowing in the streets from protest—that is the empowering spirit that has allowed Black people to turn their pain into promise. When Black people were challenged by white supremacy, with the lynching tree staring down at them, where else could they turn for hope so that their resistance would ultimately succeed?[8] It is that promise, the promise that is made real in willing to risk all, that brings a Jesus-like presence from Black people into the contemporary era. It is the promise that represents the hope to overcome white people's fear of a new history that brings the eternity of God into history.

This means, essentially, having hope in a coming kingdom that abandons notions of a pseudo-Christian faith that legitimates Christian and white superiority and coming to terms with the fact that Black people are children of God with the same worth before God as whites. It means an end to virulent stereotyping of Black aesthetic features and the abandonment of looking at Black people as commodities for capital gain and wealth attainment. It means an end to white privilege and the beginning of the theological imperative of Black liberation. The current kingdom has not yet revealed that reality, nor will it. As Joseph Washington reminds us,

---

7. James H. Cone, *The Cross and the Lynching Tree* (Maryknoll, NY: Orbis Books, 2011), 21–22.

8. Cone, *The Cross and the Lynching Tree*, 23.

> Christian ethicists generally have not been ruled by the Kingdom of God theme. Nor can they be free for the Kingdom of God until white folk religion is disintegrated, which cannot be accomplished apart from the concomitant deghettoizing of all Negroes.[9]

Washington's words from over five decades ago still ring true today. It is not just white racism that has guided American history from its inception, which committed white folks to an ungodly history; it is committing God and Jesus to that racism that has been its biggest theological blunder and, therefore, the juggernaut of eternity. Five decades later, we are still suffering with a faith malaise that avoids the liberation imperative! That malaise is especially pronounced in a postracial society, for it is tinged with the perception of progress. But the eternity of faith—the transforming spirit in the power of the blood—is what is still crucial in a society that needs divine presence in history. The coming kingdom is wrapped up in this transformative presence.

> For the heart of the American dynamic is religion. Thus, the full acceptance of the Negro group is the concern of the ethicists, who have been more concerned to speak within a segregating-discriminating ethos than to run the risks involved in changing it; and it must be their concern even to the extent of losing a place in the kingdom of this world for atonement in the Kingdom of God.[10]

The coming kingdom must not be guided by the traditional structures that affirm history as it is unfolding. That is only to move humanity within the structures of white privilege. Rather, history must be restructured such that an authentic encounter with the God of Black liberation can be made possible. In sum, history must be restructured in the way of Black liberation that identifies Black oppression as the cause to which God is most committed.

---

9. Joseph R. Washington, *The Politics of God* (Boston: Beacon Press, 1967), 130.

10. Washington, *The Politics of God*, 130.

The New Narrative of Death

The path of eternity rewrites the narrative of death and uses it for its continual construction of the kingdom. It begins with the recognition that both Jesus and Black people have been publicly killed. But the scandal of the gospel and what gives Black people hope for a liberated destiny are that they know the end of Jesus's suffering. They know that Jesus died a publicly humiliating death but overcame the power of death inflicted by the power brokers of his time. It is the knowledge of that historical reality by Black people that enables them to envision the coming kingdom as a similar resurrection for them from the historical death of white terror.

Public death is not just the physical lynching of one person but the symbolic lynching of human history! It contributes to the white kingdom and the existing situation. Public death is a humiliating stain on humanity for it is killing not only human beings but killing God as well! This becomes particularly significant given that the threat of death is the most frequently used means by power structures to instill fear in the oppressed—a fear that is magnified when a person is publicly executed. Thus, the struggle for the kingdom is the struggle to overcome the fear of death itself. As Berdyaev has noted,

> The fight against death is not only a personal matter, it is a "public undertaking." It is not only my death, but the death of all, which sets me a problem. Victory not only over the fear of death but over death itself is the realization of personality. The realization of personality is impossible in the finite, it presupposes the infinite, not quantitative infinity but qualitative, i.e., eternity.[11]

In Jesus's life, we see death as the crucible of life and, as such, a way to the eternal reality of God. In other words, God's dying in Jesus is a qualitative death in that it was a death that came in the way of eternally exposing an unjust society. This represents martyrdom

---

11. Berdyaev, *Slavery and Freedom*, 252.

and more. For not only does one die for the cause of human liberation, as Jesus did, but through that death one also announces to the world that the cause of human liberation is God's cause. As God overcame the death that the power structure of his time leveled on him, so too will Black people overcome the qualitative death placed on them and move this world closer to the true kingdom. Thus, it is qualitative death—death in the way of liberation—that spiritually transforms death into the crane that lifts humanity out of its oppressive history and prepares history for the eternal reign of God.

> Victory over the fear of death is the victory of spiritual personality over the biological individual. But this does not mean the separation of the immortal spiritual principle, from the mortal human principle, but the transformation of the whole man.[12]

Victory over the fear of death is the transformation of the whole human through oppressed humanity. It is the victory of "spiritual personality" that allows us to overcome the historical fear of death thereby rendering oppressive rule spiritually powerless. For it is the power of death that is the last obstacle to a liberated humanity.

In Alex Haley's *Roots*, no one exemplified the fear associated with death more than Fiddler. Throughout his life, he demonstrated quintessential Uncle Tom behavior, genuflecting to slave owners and rendering absurd any attempts on the part of Blacks to escape. He, like many slaves, was overwhelmed by the widespread presence of slave patrols and posses that had a high success rate in capturing escaped slaves. More importantly, he had witnessed firsthand the public, merciless floggings and even the cutting off of the foot of Kunta Kinta for seeking to escape. Fear was real and understandable! But since he had been on that plantation most of his life, the younger slaves knew that he was familiar with the layout of the surrounding area and sought his assistance several times in leading the way to the nearest escape corridor. Not only

---

12. Berdyaev, *Slavery and Freedom*, 252.

did he consistently refuse, but he encouraged other slaves to abandon notions of freedom in this world and to get comfortable with being a slave from cradle to grave. But when he saw the public hanging of a close friend, his conscience overrode his fear of death; and, as he held the dead slave in his hand after cutting him down, he, in a trembling, determined voice, proclaimed, "Ah'right, I's leads da way!"[13]

What happened to Fiddler? He truly underwent a spiritual transformation. Death, the most powerful deterrent to liberating activity, was no longer able to keep Fiddler in bondage. Historical indoctrination had been trumped by spiritual transformation. No longer was Fiddler's physical body more important to him than the freedom of his people. Historical reality had become so unbearable, even the fear of physical death, that the fear of retribution from a white God could not keep him from his date with destiny. It was at that point that Fiddler understood that he was involved in a process that would outlive him. But even if it did not outlive him and Black people were still slaves today, he still had enough of the immediate treatment of Black people to "run on and see what the end gon' be."[14]

In a similar vein, the same level of conscience was exhibited by the three Hebrew men in the Book of Daniel. Tyrant King Nebuchadnezzar had constructed an idol image and demanded that the three Hebrew men abandon their God, bow down, and worship the idol god or face the fiery furnace. The response from the men is classic, "If our God whom we serve is able to deliver us from the furnace of blazing fire and out of your hand, O king, let him deliver us. But if not, be it known to you, O king, that we will not serve your gods and we will not worship the golden statue that you have set up" (Dan 3:17–18). Therein lies the risk of faith. The mystery of God meets us in nondeterminative history, but it also meets us in determinative revelation. In other words, the mystery

---

13. Alex Haley, *Roots: The Saga of an American Family* (Boston, MA: Da Capo Press, 2014), 481.

14. Haley, *Roots*, 485.

of God meets us in a history of acute injustice but champions the cause of the victims of that injustice.

To this end, like the Hebrew men, Fiddler had met the God of Black liberation. He was no longer held captive by the whip or by a white God. He was willing to take the risk of faith in the God of Black liberation because he had become spiritually transformed to bring the eternity of God's liberation into history so that history might be transformed. In short, "the Spirit of the Lord was upon him," the same as it was with the Hebrew men and with Jesus. They were willing to risk their lives for the possibility that their deaths may not have been redemptive but solely a purely physical death with no transformative possibilities. That is the scandal of faith!

The same is true for the lives of Black people since they touched foot on American soil. We are not going to serve the God of white supremacy. Our allegiance is with the God of Black liberation. We are on the battlefield for our Lord, not the God of white supremacy, and we have been persuaded that our God will deliver us from these idolatrous hands. But even if our God does not deliver us, we are not going to serve this God! This God is of the Antichrist, not Christ. This God causes history to stagnate and does not move it to its liberating end. The God of white supremacy cannot deliver us from this evil. Only the God of Black liberation can do that! We have found that the suffering of Jesus reveals his blackness, for Jesus is able to fully understand what it is like to be Black in a racist country. The white Jesus is more familiar with a country club than with the holds of ships and an auction block and does not know what it is like to be lynched for being accused of raping a white woman or for being an uppity nigger. The white Jesus does not know what it is like to be a victim of a public death simply because a person wants to be free. The white Jesus only knows what it is like to carry out such acts. It is that solidarity in common experience of oppression for Jesus and Black people that renders Jesus's whiteness useless and renders Jesus's blackness the assurance that the kingdom is still coming.

This is why Black people testify as to how God is their "shelter from a stormy blast" and the one who "prepared a table for them in the presence of their enemies with an overflowing cup." Paul states, "To this day I have had help from God, and so I stand here, testifying to both small and great, saying nothing but what the prophets and Moses said would take place: that the Messiah must suffer, and that, by being the first to rise from the dead, he would proclaim light both to our people and to the Gentiles" (Acts 26:22–23). And on that stead, the truth of the gospel is prophesied and realized—that the Messiah would suffer in a racist world and establish the paradigm for redemptive suffering; a suffering in the way of liberation.

But because of this paradigm, the Messiah would be the first to be resurrected and to overcome the death of an oppressive world. In Jesus's resurrection, public death lost its stronghold over oppressed existence, and the mental trauma associated with that oppression became transfigured into a dogged wherewithal to be either free or dead. This is how the common experience of the suffering of Jesus and Black people made the God of Jesus Christ the God of Black liberation. As Jones states,

> The human act of the Black religious quest is a turning to God, by which act of turning, human beings become aware of themselves at the highest possible level of self-awareness. This is so simply because in such an encounter, God has addressed them. Black people cannot talk about liberation, freedom, and salvation within history unless they include the God of their eschatological future, to whom they turn in order to become whatever they shall be.[15]

They shall be free because the God of Black liberation has addressed them in their condition through God's becoming one with them in the redemptive suffering of Jesus, making him *the liberated one* and Black people *the liberated people*.

---

15. Major J. Jones, *The Color of God: The Concept of God in Afro-American Thought* (Macon, GA: Mercer University Press, 1987), 23.

God is related to a future both as the "now" and the "not yet" that cannot be derived apart from God. In the Black religious experience, the seeker must perceive God as being future as well as present. It must be so, if God is to be the God of the Black person's ultimate quest. In this sense, God is at one with the struggle of the oppressed.[16]

It is this rugged faith in the assurance of God's adoption of the cause of Black liberation that sustains Black people in the oppressive "now," knowing that the eternity of freedom will unmistakably reveal itself in the "not yet."

Run Away and Get to the North

Finally, the path of eternity focuses our attention "north." It does so to inform us that not only does a better world exist but that it is synonymous with the coming kingdom. This is not a better world that is longed for after physical death. Rather, this better world roots itself in human history. Thus, the new world both announces the beginning of a liberated world in history and also denounces the otherworldly eschatology of white Christianity employed to make Black people comfortable with earthly oppression. It is a new world, "I saw a new heaven and a new earth; for the first heaven and the first earth had passed away" (Rev 21:1). The first heaven and first earth are of the old world, the white world. The Book of Revelation announces its death; and, because it has no redemptive value for humanity, it will die and remain dead! But John notes a new reality coming from the "north."

> And I saw the holy city, the new Jerusalem, coming down out of heaven from God, prepared as a bride adorned for her husband. And I heard a loud voice from the throne saying,
> "See, the home of God is among mortals.
> He will dwell with them;
> they will be his peoples,

---

16. Jones, *The Color of God*, 23.

> and God himself will be with them;
> he will wipe every tear from their eyes.
> Death will be no more;
> mourning and crying and pain will be no more,
> for the first things have passed away." (Rev 21:2–4)

The coming kingdom is the New Jerusalem, and it comes not out of a mythical sky but is created in the upward (north) Spirit of God and descends into human history. The New Jerusalem is coming to human history and is created by God and humans who are committed to a liberated world. It will not be fettered by the trappings of white racism, or any other ism that holds humans in bondage. The New Jerusalem does not have a racist God, nor does it encourage humans to make value judgments against other human beings because of differences in complexion, gender, religious faith, or sexuality. It is a world that embraces the divine Spirit in every human being!

The New Jerusalem already exists in the Spirit of the God of Black liberation, but it still has to be realized in history. The God of Black liberation will no longer allow Black people to be duped by a white Christian leader and a milquetoast, pious Jesus. The Spirit of God is accompanying Black people to the establishment of the kingdom "in the fullness of time," not at the end of time. Such an event requires constant human activity and is brought to fulfillment by the God of Black liberation.

> The end of history is an event of existential time. And at the same time we must not think of this event as being outside history. The end of history, which is accomplished in existential time, happens both "in the next world," and "in this world."[17]

In other words, the next world happens not in a heaven that may or may not exist but is, rather, the order of human relations—liberated human relationships—formed in the venue of this world.

---

17. Berdyaev, *Slavery and Freedom*, 264.

The venue has already been physically created; now the order of human relationships must be created! In this sense, social and historical struggles are not just hobbies to fill in the time of our lives until death but rather accede with the four men with leprosy who reasoned during a great famine, "Why should we sit here until we die?" (2 Kgs 7:3). It is the divine collaboration between those committed to human liberation and the God of Black liberation. Each is dependent on the other for fulfillment. Humans cannot accomplish the kingdom on their own, and the God of Black liberation is not a panacea God who swoops down in history, touches the earth with a magic wand, and completely transfigures society. God is a co-struggling partner with the oppressed in bringing the kingdom to earth.

> An active relation to the end of history presupposes a more or less prolonged period of change in the structure of consciousness, a spiritual and social revolution even in historical time, which cannot be brought about by human efforts only, but also cannot be achieved without human effort or by passive waiting. The outpouring of the Spirit, which changes the world, is the activity of the spirit in man itself.[18]

It is a spirit that is posited in humanity by God to ignite a social revolution—a spirit posited by the God of Black liberation insofar as God is intimately acquainted with the inequality and the traumatic suffering of Black people and instills in them a desire to end their oppressive history.

The love ethic of nonretaliatory freedom has been evident in the Black prophetic radical tradition of Frederick Douglass, Harriet Tubman, Ida B. Wells Barnett, Marcus Garvey, Fannie Lou Hamer, Unita Blackwell, Jo Ann Robinson, and Martin Luther King Jr., just to name a few. The God of Black liberation, in the spirit of Jesus's own suffering and death, had God's hand on them throughout their public careers, bringing about a genuine love ethic that saw the Spirit of God in every human being while using

---

18. Berdyaev, *Slavery and Freedom*, 265.

their lives as a human sacrifice to ignite Black people's drive to freedom as the highest expression of that love, knowing the threat they would become to the white power structure.

In essence, they were saying to whites that we love you so much that we will not allow your racist understanding of love to be the norm of the nation in the coming kingdom. Rather, that norm will be guided by the love of God, who has no affinity for chattel or human division between inferior and superior, Black and white. For what you do not understand about the gospel is that you may be able to destroy my body and silence it forever, but you will never be able to destroy the Spirit of God moving in Black people in every generation. Your bigotry will prove ineffective as Black people move ever closer to a kingdom on earth that is vastly different from your kingdom.

The day of the New Jerusalem is coming from the north! It frees Black people to be used by the God of Black liberation to reveal the true kingdom to the nation and world. The New Jerusalem will no longer be possessed of fearful and insecure human beings nor of those whose will to power and xenophobia drive them to create artificial categories to exploit human differences. The New Jerusalem will mark the end of Black people who are fearful and insecure because of white terror; in the spirit of Nicodemus, they will become "born again" and stand up to white rule masquerading as democracy. They will demand the freedom that the God of Black liberation has created—a demand by Black people made possible by the path of eternity that God has created to liberate those once muted but who now have loud voices yearning to be free. In short, the Black quest for full humanity is as eternal as God's reign.

Authority over the earth does not belong to white men. The decision of granting those rights has been made by God. No group of humans has the right to say, "Deny," when God has said, "Grant!" As Joseph Washington reminds us,

> The Kingdom of God does not presuppose Christian economics, Christian politics, Christian technology. The Kingdom of God *does* presuppose the acceptance and equality of all human

groups by each human group within each and every socio-cultural pattern. The division of Negroes and whites in America is a direct contradiction of the Kingdom of God.[19]

In light of that division, the God of Black liberation calls us all to the task of Black liberation. This call does not mean showing one group of humans more favor than another. Yet because the suffering of Black people has been so acutely disproportionate, the God of Black liberation identifies with that suffering, seeking its amelioration. So significant was that suffering that God became Jesus and identified with the voiceless of first-century Palestine.

The good news of the gospel means that same identity lies with the cause of Black liberation today! God is in the bowels of Black oppression guiding Black people to the New Jerusalem. This is why they have been trying to get north ever since the time of the first slave ships. Whether it was suicides on slave ships, plantation runaways, "stealing" away to Jesus, plotting insurrections, orators and writers soundly condemning white racism's moral right to exist, repairing the grand history of African people tattered by white racists, or taking to the streets to voice righteous indignation, in all these instances the God of Black liberation has been the driving force that continually produces in Black people the existential restlessness with racial subordination. Blacks have been forever trying to get north, to escape to a higher state of being, a higher state of conscience, a higher state of unrequited freedom, to the New Jerusalem. Staying in a continual state of prayer for God to keep them "forever in thy path," they are buoyed by the words, "then let the sail be bent to the main-mast, and let the ship of the Faith, issuing out from the harbor where it lies rotting and anchored, sail before the wind towards the furtherest star, indifferent to the darkness around it."[20] That "furtherest" star is also the North Star—the star of freedom, the star of the kingdom. So run away children, and get to the north!

---

19. Washington, *The Politics of God*, 129.
20. Washington, *The Politics of God*, 142.

Index

accommodationism
    influence on Black church, 21, 22
    racial, and Black freedom, 19–25
African culture, depictions of, 41–45
African/Black history
    and Black self-image, 44, 45
    and conversion experience, 40–45
Alexander, Michelle, on criminalization of Blacks, 131, 132
America
    as a theologically unjust country, 109
    as two nations, 118–21, 129, 168, 169
    as a white country, 119
Amos (biblical prophet), critique of social injustice, 113–14, 117
Amos 'n' Andy, 79
apathy, as reason to avoid racial struggle, 114, 115

Baldwin, James
    on the "new" Negro, 143, 144
    on radical change in American society, 143
    on the spiritual state of the nation, 141, 142
"The Ballot or the Bullet" (Malcolm X speech), 14
baptism, and freedom of slaves, 34, 35
Barnett, Ida B. *See* Wells Barnett, Ida B.
Berdyaev, Nikolai
    on the end of history, 179, 180
    on the fight against death, 173, 174
    on freedom of God as source of human freedom, 1
    on the ideology of the bourgeois classes, 167, 168
    on transcendence and liberation, 5
Berkeley, Bishop George
    letter to colonists on baptism and freedom (1727), 34, 35, 50
    on sin as belonging to the interior life, 90
Bible, as ordaining Black enslavement, 61–63
The Birth of a Nation (D. W. Griffith), 79, 131
Black church
    creation of pious Blacks, 109

Black church (*cont.*)
   disregard for racism, 37
   as key to liberation, 151
   at odds with freedom movements, 44
   preaching in, 45, 46, 47
   role on the path to liberation, 160, 161
   similarity to white church, 36, 37, 38, 38, 39, 40
Black church leadership
   conflict with Black militants, 116, 117
   and institutional success, 115
   and a new theology of liberation, 151, 152
   opposition to social change, 115, 116
Black Jesus/Black Christ, 50–56
Black liberation, obstacles to, 143, 144
Black Lives Matter, 12, 27
Black militants
   on the American white God, 148
   and prophetic call for justice, 115–17
Black nationalists
   and separation of races, 15–17
   views of whites and God, 16
   See also Black militants; militant religion
Black theology. *See* theology, Black
Black women, and denial of right to vote, 126
blackness
   and Blacks' self-image, 80
   as cause of Black suffering, 53, 83–84, 138, 161
   as creation of God, 80
   of God, xxvii, 84, 100
   God's identification with, 7, 56, 84, 97, 100, 138
   of Jesus, 176
   white contempt for, 40, 42
Blacks
   as conscience of the nation, 23
   criminality of, 104
   dehumanization of, 13, 18, 35, 40, 55, 58, 63, 68, 79, 108, 109, 110, 122, 133, 137, 148,
   false depictions by whites, 41
   fearless approach to death, 176, 177
   as free by nature, 14–19
   as God's chosen people, 87, 88, 96
   identification with Jesus, sinner and criminal, 133
   loving their blackness, 80
   overcoming death, 173, 174
   positive reimaging of, 41
   stereotypes of, 36, 60, 80, 121, 130, 131, 168, 171
   as reflection of the image of God, xxvii, 9, 14, 36, 67, 69, 79
   subordination of, 81, 82
   as three-fifths of a person, 124
   as unfree in history, 14–19
   and use of the language of liberation, 157, 158
   as victims of racial imperialism, 54
   in view of framers of the Constitution, 118
   and white demand for Christian obedience, 60–66

and white depictions of African culture, 42, 43
Blacks and whites, disparate historical experiences, 40. *See also* America, as two nations
Blackwell, Unita, and Black prophetic tradition, 180
Brown v. Board of Education, 81

Carr, Joseph M., on equality of Blacks and whites, 10
Christ event
  as liberation of oppressed community, 76, 77
  meaning of, 142–44, 157
  and modern history, 52, 53
Christian institutions, and legitimation of white superiority, 109
Christianity, American, as obstacle to Black freedom, 30
church and state, separation of, and the white church, 150, 151
Cinque, Joseph, 110
circumcision, and Paul's message to Galatian church, 26
civil rights movement, and goal of integration, 14–17
civilization, as pretext for oppression, 86, 87, 99
Cleage, Albert, on life of Jesus as one of conflict, 74–77
Coleman, Will, and the language of liberation of American slaves, 153
Cone, James
  on affirmation of Black dignity, 133
  on the blackness of Black people, 80
  on blackness of God, xxvii
  on Christ event and modern history, 52, 53
  on Christian behavior of oppressed community, 71
  on deprivation of Black dignity, 8, 103
  on God's gift of freedom, 161
  on God's liberation of the oppressed, 139
  on historical struggle for freedom, 145
  on image of God and human freedom, 9
  on innocence of Jesus and of African Americans, 104
  on love and righteousness of God, 100
  on significance of resurrection of Jesus, 160
  on symbolism of Black, 56
  on wrath of God, 107
conversion
  as calling for Black liberation, 41
  and Christian freedom, 34–39
  as civilizing influence, 34
  and freedom of slaves, 34, 35
  and legitimation of white supremacy, 35
converts, and personal salvation, 32, 33, 34
criminal injustice system, 131, 132
criminalization, of Blacks, 129–34, 168
cross and lynching tree, 104
Cummings, George
  on religion in life of slave community, 146

Cummings, George (*cont.*)
   on resurrecting power of the Spirit in Black community, 144

Daniel (biblical book), fearless approach to death in, 175, 176
David and Goliath (biblical story), 22
death
   of Jesus and of Blacks, 173
   and the kingdom of white privilege, 165, 166
   physical, through assault on Black skin, 79
   public, 173
   spiritual, of Blacks, through imposition of white supremacy, 78
divine righteousness, and white privilege, 94
Douglas, Kelly Brown, on rebellion against social barriers to freedom, 54
Douglass, Frederick, 25
   and Black prophetic tradition, 180
   on Blacks influenced by the white God, 148
   and the language of liberation, 152
   on racist American laws, 101, 102
Dred Scott decision, 125
Du Bois, W. E. B., 25
   and the language of liberation, 152
   on racism as America's sin, 91, 93

Ebenezer Baptist Church, 48, 116
education, denial to Blacks, 94, 124, 152, 153
Ellison, Ralph, on racial blindness of whites, 121
Emerson, Michael, on racial views of white evangelicals, 120
enslavement, and present kingdom, 162
entitlement programs, as source of racial problems, 120

fear
   of death, 174
   and the struggle for liberation, 161
Fifteenth Amendment, 126
Floyd, George, lynching of, 98
Fourteenth Amendment, 126
freedom
   of all humans, 2
   as most important commandment, 70, 72
   as nature of God, 7–10, 13, 14
   See also liberation
Fugitive Slave Act (1850), 124, 125

Garnet, Henry Highland
   on Black resistance to oppression, 109–11
   on God of retributive justice, 111
   on primacy of ending Black oppression and slavery, 68–70
Garvey, Marcus, and Black prophetic tradition, 180
"Go Down Moses," and God of social reconstruction, xxiii

God
  as author of Black suffering, xiii
  of compensatory reward, xiv
  as great in power, 85, 86
  historical intervention on behalf of oppressed, 65, 136
  and human freedom, 9, 10
  identification with slaves and oppressed, 5–8, 11, 12, 28, 29, 55, 56, 65, 85–87, 95, 104, 113, 135, 138
  of personal blessings, 71, 72
  of social righteousness, 84–90
  used by white America to justify racism, 91, 92
  of the white community, illusory beliefs about, 169, 170
  of white privilege/supremacy, 40, 44, 46, 72, 96, 101, 124, 132, 139, 165, 176
  view of Black nationalists, 16
God of Black liberation, *passim*
Gutiérrez, Gustavo
  on God as liberator in history, 136, 137
  on Jesus as the source of life, 166
  on Jesus's rejection of master class, 4
  on resignation in face of history, 59, 60
  on ruling class in Latin America, 163, 164

Hacker, Andrew, on two American nations, 118–19
Hamer, Fannie Lou, and Black prophetic tradition, 180
Hammon, Jupiter
  attitude toward slavery, xvi, xvii
  image of God in poetry of, xvi
Hampton Institute (University), 20
heathenism, and African culture, 41, 42
heaven, and personal salvation for "good" behavior, xxiii, 27, 28, 67, 69, 70, 78, 81, 82, 115
heaven on earth, and white privilege, 81, 82
history
  as venue of God's coming kingdom, 167–72
  as venue of God's liberation, 136, 137, 179, 180
hope, in coming kingdom of God, 170, 171
Hopkins, Dwight
  on Black culture of resistance, 105
  on God's identification with the oppressed, 97
  on inherent freedom of Blacks, 17
hostility, of whites toward Blacks, 168–70
Howard, Josephine, on Black "stealing" ethic, 105, 106
human rights, denial to Blacks, 121, 122

"I Have a Dream" speech (Martin Luther King Jr.), 113
images of God
  atheism model, xvi–xx
  otherworldliness model, xiv–xvi

images of God (cont.)
- physical and emotional security model, xi–xiv
- social reconstruction model, xx–xxv

incarnation
- of God of Black liberation, 50, 51, 52, 53
- reality and relevance of, 78

individualism, in Black church, 39, 45, 128, 144

indoctrination, Christian, of Blacks, 38, 39

injustice, racial, and racial unrest, 145

integration, and civil rights movement, 14–17

Jackson, J. H., 48, 49

Jefferson, Thomas, on Black inferiority, 65, 66

Jesus
- assassination by religious establishment, 75, 76
- as Black African Hebrew, 50, 51
- and freedom of the oppressed, 6, 7
- God of, 8, 38, 55, 70, 87, 104, 107, 125, 127, 132, 133, 139, 144, 147, 148, 155, 166, 169, 177
- historical lynching of, 53
- and the language of liberation, 154–57
- ministry of, as threat to religious establishment, 74–76
- as revolutionary, 142
- as Second Adam, 51

Jim Crow, xii
- new Jim Crow, 131, 132

Job (biblical figure)
- on God as great in power, 85, 86
- on justice and righteousness of God, 85–87
- and physical and emotional security model of God, xiii

Johnson, James Weldon, on God of Black liberation, xxix

Jones, Major
- on divine freedom, 13
- on God and liberation of Blacks, xxvii, xxvii
- on God and the eschatological future, 177–78

justice
- American racial, 118, 124
- Black quest for, 112–17
- for Blacks, anthropological justification for, 121
- denial to Blacks, as duty to God, 124
- equal, as fraudulent claim, 128, 129

Justitia (Roman goddess), 118

King, Martin Luther, Jr.
- and Black prophetic tradition, 180
- on Black religious leadership, 48, 114, 115
- and civil rights movement, 25
- dismissal from National Baptist Convention, 48, 49
- on elusiveness of peace in American society, 92
- experience of divine presence, 112, 113

and freedom through non-
  violence, 71, 77
and the language of liberation,
  152, 157, 158
on preaching in Black church,
  47, 48
on social responsibility of Black
  church leaders, 115, 116
violation of laws of segregation,
  126
kingdom of God, coming, 162,
  163, 166, 167
and biblical revelation, 165
rooted in human history, 178,
  179
kingdom of God, present, 162,
  163
kingdom of heaven, 81, 82, 83,
  85
on earth, 89, 90

language, Christian
  deficient in denouncing Black
    oppression, 49
  as spiritual and otherworldly,
    49, 102
language, sermonic, of Black
  preachers, 46–49
language of liberation, 152–58
law(s)
  different views of Blacks and
    whites, 128
  of the nation, as extension of
    God's laws, 123, 126
  racial, and two humanities,
    108
  racist, 125, 126
  of segregation, violation of, 126
The Leopard's Spots (Thomas
  Dixon), 79, 131

liberation
  of oppressed, as will of
    God, 51. *See also* God,
    identification with slaves
    and oppressed
  sacred nature of, 145–52
  spiritual nature of, 139–45
liberation themes, and Black
  preaching, 47
liberation theologians, and
  preferential option for the
  poor, 159
L'Ouverture, Toussaint, 110
love of God
  in contemporary history, 97,
    98
  for the oppressed, 94–100.
    See also God, identification
    with slaves and oppressed
love ethic, in Black prophetic
  tradition, 180, 181
Luther, Martin
  on righteousness of God, 82
  and worldly salvation, 158,
    159
lynchings
  and deprivation of dignity,
    104
  in twentieth-century America,
    21

Malcolm X
  on human freedom, 17, 18
  and separation of races, 15
  on struggle for Black freedom,
    14–19
  understanding of religion, 18,
    19
master class, theology of, 3–5, 11
master–slave division, 3–6

Mays, Benjamin
   on African Americans'
      understandings of God, xi–
      xxv
   on Blacks as God's chosen
      people, 88
   on freedom and image of God
      in all humans, xxv
   on God's social righteousness,
      87
   on the need for a Black
      theology, 148, 149
   on negative goodness, 102
   preference for God of social
      reconstruction, xxii, xxiii
   as pre-liberation theologian,
      xxvi
   on racial strife, xxv, xxvi
   relationship with Martin
      Luther King Jr., 48
Messiah and Blacks, redemptive
   suffering of, 177
militancy, as justifiable response to
   Black oppression, 8
militant religion, xxvi, 30, 31,
   45–50, 110, 111, 148
Monk, Kaj, on the holy rage of
   Jesus, 155
Montgomery bus boycott, 48, 112
Morehouse College, 48
Moreland, Mantan, 79

Nation of Islam, 15
negative goodness (Benjamin
   Mays), xv, xvi, xvii, 102
The Negro: A Beast (Charles
   Carroll), 79
Negro, as God's most perfect
   handiwork (Benjamin
   Mays), xxv

*The Negro: A Menace to American
   Civilization* (Robert
   Shufeldt), 131
*The Negro's God as Reflected in His
   Literature* (Benjamin E.
   Mays), xi, xxvi,
neighbor, in parable of good
   Samaritan, 75
new covenant, and freedom of
   God, 25–31
New Jerusalem, and coming king-
   dom of God, 179–82
"north," symbolic meaning of, 85,
   88, 89, 90, 178, 182
Notes on the State of Virginia
   (Thomas Jefferson), 65

obedience
   Black, as the divine will, 61,
      63, 64
   and Black liberation, 74–80
   Christian, and human libera-
      tion, 66, 67
   to God of Black liberation, 57
   and liberation, 60
   as obstacle to Black humanity,
      61
   and passive resignation, 59, 63,
      80
"Oh Freedom," and God of social
   reconstruction, xxiii
otherworldliness, and Black
   church, 45, 46, 47, 71, 72

pastors, white and Black, silence
   on racism, sexism, and
   poverty, 36, 37
Paul (apostle)
   instructions for slaves and
      masters, 57, 58

on love (*agape*) and pursuit of
    freedom, 29, 30
message of freedom to Galatian
    church, 26, 27
on obeying governmental
    authorities, 123, 124
on righteousness of God, 83
Paul, Bishop Nathaniel
    on Black rejection of slavery,
    10
    on God's righteousness, 89
Payne, Bishop Daniel, and
    "atheist" model of God,
    xvii, xviii, xix
Plessy v. Ferguson (1896 Supreme
    Court decision), xii, 21, 23,
    125
police, killing of Blacks, 28, 98
political institutions, and spiritual
    state of the nation, 141,
    142
political system, American, and
    racist laws, 101, 104, 126,
    127
preaching
    in Black church, 45, 46, 47
    on the plantation, 46
prophets (biblical), confrontation
    with oppression, 65
punishment of Blacks, for
    violating racist laws/slave
    codes, 124, 127

racial caste, white maintenance of,
    9, 13, 21, 93, 94, 101,
racism
    as America's greatest sin, 91,
    92–96
    Christian, and God's
    liberation, 138

of Christian theology, 86, 87
dismissal as one sin among
    many, 96
and divine righteousness,
    90–94
and God's identification with
    Blacks, 140
legal sanctioning of, xii
in postslavery context, 98
and religious institutions, 107
rebellion
    against oppression of Blacks,
    66
    against social barriers to Black
    freedom, 54
religion
    disillusionment with, 78
    formalistic, 30
    in life of slave community, 146
    as path of freedom, 18
religious personalism, of white
    church, 122
resurrection, as a sign of liberation
    to Black community, 56,
    70, 77, 80, 137, 138, 156,
    159, 160, 173, 177
retribution
    and God's love, 98
    as theme of militant Black
    leadership, 111
    for whites' treatment of Blacks,
    99, 110, 158
righteousness
    and identification with the
    oppressed, 83, 84
    and kingdom of heaven, 81, 82
righteousness of God, and wrath
    of God, 101–7
Robinson, Jo Ann, and Black
    prophetic tradition, 180

Roosevelt, President Theodore, and Booker T. Washington at White House, 20, 21
Roots (Alex Haley), 23, 174
   and the fear of death, 174, 175

sacred and profane, in African culture, 146, 147
salvation
   otherworldly, in white theology, 158, 159
   personal, 32, 33, 34
   through submission to oppression, 86
   as this-worldly, 137
salvation of the world, through Black liberation, 158–61
segregation, and unequal treatment, 168
Segundo, Juan Luis, on Western liturgy, 36
separate but equal, 125
separation of races, and Black nationalist groups, 15–17
Sessions, Jeff (former attorney general), and nation's laws as God's laws, 123–24, 128
shallow pragmatism, Benjamin Mays on, xiv, xv
slave class, theology of, 4
slave codes, 108, 124
slave trade, xi–xiii, 12, 58, 98, 108
slavery, xi, xii, xiii, xvi
   as Christian stewardship, 34
   as creation of God, 63
   and denial of freedom, 3
   as eternal institution, 34
   in Greco-Roman Empire, 58, 67
   as human institution, 64
   and obedience to the commandments, 68, 69
   as racist institution, 125
   theological justification for, 57, 58
slaves
   conversion of, for economic exploitation, 42, 63
   education of, xviii
   God's identification with, 8. *See also* God, identification with slaves and oppressed
   "good," 81
   and the language of liberation, 153, 154
   obedient, 61, 62, 63
   violence against, 98
Smith, Christian, on racial views of white evangelicals, 120
Sobrino, Jon, on the ultimacy of reality, 140
social responsibility, avoidance of, forced on Blacks, 101, 102
social righteousness, and God of Black liberation, 84–90
Sölle, Dorothee
   on freedom of humans, 2
   on oppression of existing world order, 5
Spirit of God, and liberation imperative, 139–44
spirituality
   as communal, 143, 144
   white Christian, 140, 141
   white individualistic, 144
spirituals
   and God of social reconstruction, xxiii
   and repudiation of the world, xxi

"stealing" ethic, 105, 129, 130
Stepin Fetchit, 79
suffering
    as key to salvation for Blacks and whites, xx
    merited/unmerited, of Jesus and Blacks, 170, 171
    as revelation of blackness of Jesus, 176
Sundays, celebration of, in slave community, 46, 47

theology
    Black, characteristics, 148, 149
    Black, and liberating activity, 147
    racist, 27
    white, on Black inferiority, 146–49
    white, and Black subservience, 61–64
    white, and otherworldly salvation, 158, 159
    white, and racism, 54, 55
    of white privilege, 73, 85
Thirteenth Amendment, 126
Thoreau, Henry David, on civil disobedience, 126
Tolstoy, Leo
    on disobeying laws, 126, 127
    on universal love, 99, 100
Tubman, Harriet, 25
    and Black prophetic tradition, 180
Turner, Henry McNeal, 25
Turner, Nat, 110
    and freedom through violence, 71
    insurrection of, 85
Tuskegee Institute (University), 20

ultimacy of reality, 140
universalism, of God, 88, 122

Vesey, Denmark, 85, 110
violence
    against Blacks, 92, 127, 169, 171
    and liberation of Blacks from oppression, 71

Waiting for the Barbarians (J. M. Coetzee), 163
Walker, David
    on absence of Blacks from political and economic institutions, 121
    on consequences of oppression of Blacks, 12
    disdain for white Christianity, 149
    on ending oppression of Blacks, 65, 66
    on treatment of Blacks by whites, 99
Washington, Booker T.
    on Blacks' maintaining a Protestant work ethic, 20
    racial accommodationism of, 20–25
Washington, Joseph
    challenge to white Christian ethicists, 90
    on coming kingdom of God, 171, 172
    on deghettoizing of Negroes, 24
    on equality and the kingdom of God, 181, 182
    on *kairos* moment for confronting racism, 23, 24

Washington, Joseph (*cont.*)
   on Negro folk religion, 37
   on Negro rise to white middle class, 38, 39
   on racism as one sin among many, 96
Washington, Madison, 110
Wells Barnett, Ida B., and Black prophetic tradition, 25, 180
West Africans, and slave trade, 58
Wheatley, Phyllis
   attitude toward slavery, xvi, xvii
   image of God in poetry of, xvi
   renunciation of Africa's goodness, xvi, xvii
white church
   opposition to Black freedom, 27, 28
   support for slavery and segregation, 149–51
white evangelicals, racial views of, 119, 120
white people
   as mediators between God and Blacks, 63, 68
   as only humanity in colonial life, 108, 109
   opposition to Black freedom movements, 27
   racial blindness of, 119, 121
   as source of Black suffering, 122
   use of the Bible to support slavery, 61, 62, 63
   view of good Black behavior, 67, 68, 69
   See also white privilege; white superiority/supremacy
white power, manipulation of, for Black advancement, 22
white privilege, xx
   and American political system, 101
   and divine will, 82
   and racism, 96
white Southerners, belief in God's favor, 162, 163
white superiority/supremacy
   and American political system, 103
   and Black freedom movements, 27
   and conversion, 35
   and divine wisdom, 43
   God as mastermind of, 72, 109
   and the kingdom of God, 163–67
   myth of, 92, 107
   as natural order, 27
   saying no to, 11–13
   white theology in support of, 146–51
women, denial of ministry to, in Black church, 37
Woodson, Carter G., on God's love for all humans, 95
wrath of God, 101–7
   and the day of vindication, 106

www.ingramcontent.com/pod-product-compliance
Lightning Source LLC
Chambersburg PA
CBHW070842160426
43192CB00012B/2276